THE WEB LEARNING FIELDBOOK

THE WEB LEARNING FIELDBOOK

Using the World Wide Web to Build Workplace Learning Environments

Valorie Beer
Foreword by Sueann Ambron
Web Templates by Thor Anderson

Jossey-Bass
Pfeiffer

Copyright © 2000 by Jossey-Bass/Pfeiffer
ISBN: 0-7879-5023-8

Library of Congress Cataloging-in-Publication Data

Beer, Valorie.
    The web learning fieldbook: using the world wide web to build workplace learning environ-
ments / Valorie Beer; foreword by Sueann Ambron.
      p. cm.
    Includes bibliographical references and index.
    ISBN 0–7879–5023–8 (pbk.: alk. paper)
    1. Employees—Training of—Computer network resources. 2. Employees—Training of—
Computer-assisted instruction. 3. World Wide Web (Information retrieval system) I. Title.
    HF5549.5.T7 B415 2000
    658.3'12404'02854678—dc21

                                                 99–050487

Printed in the United States of America

Published by

350 Sansome Street, 5th Floor
San Francisco, California 94104-1342
(415) 433-1740; Fax (415) 433-0499
(800) 274-4434; Fax (800) 569-0443

Visit our website at: www.pfeiffer.com

Acquiring Editor: Matthew Holt
Director of Development: Kathleen Dolan Davies
Developmental Editor: Rachel Livsey
Editor: Hilary Powers
Senior Production Editor: Judith Hibbard
Manufacturing Supervisor: Becky Carreño
Interior Design Adaptation: Gene Crofts
Cover Design: Blue Design (www.bluedes.com)
Illustrations/Web Templates: Thor Anderson
Compositor: Leigh McLellan

Printing   10 9 8 7 6 5 4 3 '2 1

 This book is printed on acid-free, recycled stock that meets or exceeds the minimum GPO
and EPA requirements for recycled paper.

CONTENTS

PART TWO: PREPARING TO USE THE WEB FOR LEARNING   21

PART THREE: WEB LEARNING DESIGN STUDIO   69

LIST OF EXHIBITS

FOREWORD

Writing a book about Web learning is like catching a cloud. The cloud is moving across the sky, constantly changing form, and can be seen in new light each moment. This book is coming at a time when it is useful to take a snapshot of Web learning and analyze what we have and how to use it. Both business and education are asking questions about the use of the Internet for learning. This book provides timely answers and topics for reflection.

Web learning is a subject of great interest to me. As the president of Avulet, a Silicon Valley company creating and delivering Web learning for network professionals, I grapple every day with the learning aspects of the Web environment in content development, delivery, and refinement. The guidelines, ideas, and questions in this book have been useful to my company's instructional designers, Web designers, and applications engineers. Not only does every idea in the *Web Learning Fieldbook* apply to our business, it also applies to product marketing groups who are trying to get training out with short product life cycles, to professionals who are trying to figure out how to stay on top of their field, and to training professionals who are trying to reach a worldwide audience.

I have known Valorie Beer for ten years. In that time she has been at the forefront of technology and education, first at Xerox, then at Apple, and more recently at Netscape and E*TRADE. She has always been where the action is. She is a skilled instructional designer and analytical thinker with practical advice. Readers of this book are fortunate to have such an experienced guide.

The subject of this book—Web learning—should be of intense interest to many people. Who knows what will come after the Web? But in the meantime, there is no doubt that there is significant interest when governments and venture capitalists alike are talking about big investments in learning on the Internet.

The treatment of Web learning in this book is extraordinarily sensible. The *Web Learning Fieldbook* makes compelling arguments to support its conclusions. Valorie always comes back to the learner: "What do your learners need and is there a way that the Web can help?" "Do you learn this way?" "Do you know anyone who does?"

The *Web Learning Fieldbook* is a snapshot in time of the changing clouds of learning on the Internet. Valorie has provided not only an observation of what is going on, but a careful analysis of what needs to be done by people who are designing Web learning. The book illuminates what is important today and provides thought-provoking ideas and techniques for what will be important for Web learning in the future.

Sueann Ambron
Founder of Apple's Multimedia Lab
and Paramount's Media Kitchen
September 1999
Portola Valley, California

PREFACE

The World Wide Web is the universal interface to the world's digital library. As such, it has great potential for education because it gives learners, instructors, and instructional designers unprecedented access to information and to the experts who create it. However, it is imperative that you think carefully about using the Web in your workplace learning environment so that it does not become just another medium that promised (and failed) to save education, to dramatically reduce training costs, to provide just-in-time training, and to satisfy all the other expectations that educators and learners have had about technology.

This book will help you set your own expectations for what the Web can do for learners in your company. It will then help you bring those expectations to reality by guiding you in the creation of learning environments that make appropriate use of the Web. Throughout the book, the focus is on defining what your learners need and then using the Web to get them there, rather than choosing the Web first and then trying to get your learners to use it. Four interviews with Web-learning experts give you real-world guidance on creating your Web learning environment.

After reading this book and using the tools and templates that it contains, you will be able to critically evaluate how much of your learning environment should be on the Web. You can then create just those pieces that need to be there. This book will also help you make your case for—or perhaps against—Web learning, just in case you are being pushed to use the Web to deliver all training in your company.

Who Should Read This Book

This book is for training managers, instructional designers, instructors, and human performance support specialists in workplace settings. That is, the focus of this book is not on using the Web for K–12 or higher education, although those audiences would find that many of the principles and tools in the book are applicable to their institutions.

This book includes several assumptions:

- You have already made the choice, or have been given the mandate, to use the Web as part of the learning environment in your company.
- You are familiar with the basic technology and terminology of the Web, such as HTML, HTTP, and URL (if not, see the Glossary at the end of this book).
- You have some experience in creating workplace training and performance support tools.

The book also assumes that your main responsibility is creating the learning aspects of the Web environment rather than designing the user interface and navigation, creating the graphics, or maintaining the Web server. While this book refers to these latter tasks, its focus is on creating the learning experiences that your users will access through the Web.

What This Book Is About

This book is about using the Web to create environments in which your employees or customers can learn new skills. The emphasis is on learning; that is, on how your audience will transform information into new behaviors. Because you are in a workplace setting, this book focuses on using the Web to help people develop their skills, to do something useful with the information that the Web holds. Therefore, this book is more about how to develop interactions between the learner and the Web, and less about presentation and delivery of information.

Too often in the workplace, discussions of training emphasize transmission and delivery, that is, what the instructional designer and instructor need to do with the media. In contrast, this book uses *learning* instead of *training*, helping you take the perspective of the user of your Web learning environment. Instead of the question, How can you teach using the Web? this book asks, What do your learners need, and is there a way that the Web can help them get it?

This book is also about looking critically at what you want to put on the Web for your learners. Much computer-based training is simple page-turning that requires the learner to sit for hours in front of a screen. Much of the available Web-based training is no different. However, easy access to a plethora of multimedia and human resources does not mean that learning will happen. Therefore, at several places in this book you will be asked to stop for a reality check about what you want to put on the Web.

Web Learning Reality Check!

- Do you learn this way?
- Do you know anyone who does?
- Could you learn what you are expecting others to learn from your Web site?

℘ ℘ ℘ ℘ ℘ ℘

In short, this book is about helping you to keep learning in mind as you design educational Web environments, and to remember that flashy multimedia does not guarantee learning.

What This Book Is Not About

There are four topics related to Web learning that this book does not cover.

- This book does not review or describe how to use the plethora of commercial tools available for creating Web-based training. There is a list of these tools in Appendix A at the end of the book. This book is about what you need to consider regardless of what Web site creation tools you use.

- This is not a book on how to choose media for educational purposes. The Web is not a single medium, nor is it appropriate (in most cases) to use it as the sole medium of instruction. The Web is a player of various media, and you need to make media decisions before you begin assembling the learning environment of which the Web is one part.

- This is not a book on instructional design, although Chapter Six strongly recommends that you choose an instructional design strategy and stick to it. A coherent organizational design will help you keep your focus on learning and avoid getting distracted by the Web's technology—but the topic is too complex to combine an in-depth treatment with the other subject matter here. See Appendix C for resources on instructional design.

- This book does not cover content or document management, although distribution, version control, access rights, and security are important issues. Chapter Six lists some resources for you in these areas.

Chapters at a Glance

After the first two introductory chapters, the book is divided into two major sections—preparing to use the Web for learning, and the Web learning design studio. If you have not yet used the Web for learning, the first section will help you analyze your company's learning environment, and will give you some practical tips on the strengths and drawbacks of using the Web for learning. If you already have some experience with the Web, you can go to the design studio and begin working on your own Web learning environment. To find out which chapters you will need, you can start by reading the chapter objectives. Each chapter also has a "To Learn More About" section that gives you references for topics not covered in depth in the chapter.

Part One: The World Wide Web's Role in Learning

This part gives you a basic introduction to how the World Wide Web is currently used for teaching and learning.

Chapter One: Why Web Learning? This first introductory chapter presents statistics and commentary on the growth of the World Wide Web. It also describes why this technological phenomenon is important to teaching and learning.

Chapter Two: How the Web Is Used for Learning. This second introductory chapter describes and gives examples of how the Web is currently used to support learning, including as a catalog of courses, a delivery vehicle for content and collaborative learning, a resource center for research and discussion about using the Web for learning, and as a tools source for downloading or purchasing software to create Web learning environments.

Part Two: Preparing to Use the Web for Learning

The three chapters in this section present tasks for you to do and ideas for you to consider before you start creating your Web learning environment.

Chapter Three: Learning Environments. This chapter suggests that you avoid using the Web as the single learning environment for your workplace. Many examples of "Web-based learning" are simply the content of hours of classroom or computer-based training that have been converted into HTML and put on a Web site. The chapter reiterates the questions, Do you learn this way? and Do you know anyone who does? In this chapter you will find guidelines and tools for figuring out what your learners need to learn, what their work environment is like, and what instructional design and media will work best for them. You will also find an interview with a Web-learning practitioner who will give you some real-world hints about assessing your environment's readiness for Web learning. The point of the chapter: find out what your learners need before you rush to the Web (or to any other medium).

Chapter Four: Communities of Learners. This chapter reviews the rich body of research and practical experience on the importance of building a community of learners, teachers, and experts. It shows the fallacy of believing that learning can occur by sitting a solitary individual in front of a computer screen. This reinforces the point that hours of point-and-click "self-paced training" is not a fruitful use of the Web. The chapter concludes with a preview of some of the ways that the Web can be used to create and support a community of learners.

Chapter Five: Pros and Cons of Using the Web for Learning. Now that you have investigated the learners' environment and thought about the community of learners that you want to create, you are almost ready to begin building learning for the Web. However, there are some caveats to be aware of, and this chapter presents seven of them that you should consider before you start to work on a Web learning environment.

Part Three: Web Learning Design Studio

The six chapters in this section contain tools, templates, and checklists that will get you started on creating your Web learning environment.

Chapter Six: Organizing Content for Web Learning. What kinds of content will you be presenting on the Web, and how will you organize it? This chapter suggests that more than just factual knowledge can be presented on the Web. You will find examples of different kinds of content and how they might be organized. The chapter makes a strong recommendation that you choose a consistent way of organizing the content (a "content architecture"), as how you organize the content will influence the user interface design and navigation of your site. The chapter also suggests that you provide ways for your learners to contribute content themselves. Because you cannot expect your instructional designers to be able to gather all the possible content or keep it current, you will need to provide a way for learners to contribute content that they have found or created.

Chapter Seven: Presentation Strategies for Web Learning. This chapter begins with the warning that information is not instruction, and that simply putting up flashy graphics does not constitute creating a learning environment. Several strategies for presenting material with varying amounts of learner control are suggested. Because simulations are a popular way of presenting material on the Web, this chapter also includes an interview with a Web learning simulation expert, who describes some of the uses of Web simulations and what it takes to build them.

Chapter Eight: Web Learning Activities. This chapter acknowledges that you cannot use the Web for the hands-on learning activities required for mastering many subjects. (This is not a problem, obviously, if you are teaching any subject that involves working with computers or configuring devices such as networks through computers. In those cases, the Web is the perfect "hands-on" environment.) However, because of its collaborative aspects, the Web can facilitate new thinking and not just information dissemination. This chapter describes how you can use the Web for exploratory and collaborative learning activities, and concludes with an interview with a designer of structured Web-based discussion groups that have learning as their primary goal.

Chapter Nine: Assessing Web Learning and Web Learning Environments. This chapter presents some ideas on new ways of assessing learning and providing feedback and remediation that are now possible because of the Web.

Chapter Ten: Using Instructors in Web Learning Environments. This chapter addresses an area that has been largely overlooked in the rush to get learning materials to the Web: how to involve the instructor in the Web learning experience, either in the traditional classroom or in the new Web-based "virtual classroom." Your company probably spends too much time and money keeping classroom instructors current on new developments, such as new products. By using the Web as an in-classroom resource, you can ensure that your instructors have the latest information at their fingertips. If your instructors know where to find information on a Web site that was created for their class, then they do not need to keep so much quickly outdated knowledge in their heads; they can concentrate on helping their learners instead. This chapter also discusses how to use the Web for asynchronous virtual classrooms, and concludes with an interview with a provider of instructor-led Web-based training.

Chapter Eleven: A Summary of Learning and Technical Considerations for Web Learning Environments. This chapter gives you guidelines and advice for putting all the learning elements together in your Web site. Good examples of existing public Web sites are included for you to visit and analyze.

The book concludes with five Appendixes—a list of Web sites that contain tools for building Web learning environments; a discussion of Distance Learning/Local Learning by Libby Bishop, research scientist at the Institute for Research on Learning; a complete set of screen captures of the images provided in the Web site; a references section; and a recommended reading and browsing list. There is also a Glossary that defines Internet and instructional design terms. The Web site can be found at:

www.pfeiffer.com/beer.html

This Web site includes sample learning environments as a guide in creating your own (the screen captures for these are in Appendix C), links to related sites, and electronic templates and tools for customizing and downloading.

Valorie Beer
November 1999
Palo Alto, California

ACKNOWLEDGMENTS

Many friends and colleagues supported my writing with their suggestions, insights, and practical experiences in teaching, learning, and using the Web. My first and deepest thanks to Thor Anderson, who let me talk him into creating all of the Web tools for the book. Thor is that rare combination, an educator who knows how to hack—that is, how to get the most out of a programming language—and this book would not have been a "field guide" without his talents in both areas. Jamie Dinkelacker, Peter Henschel, Howard Lewis, Patrick O'Hare, Mark Ouyang, Mitch Plott, Dan Russell, and Mark Stern read early drafts and pointed me to many of the books, articles, and Web sites cited in the book. My managers, Mike Major and Kandis Malefyt at Netscape and Jerry Dark at E*TRADE, enthusiastically supported the double life I led while I tried to write the book and hold down a job at the same time. Nancy Flanagan, Dan Leonard, Libbi Lepow, and Allison Rossett were cheerleaders extraordinaire, and gave sage advice on life, the book, and everything. Matt Holt and Rachel Livsey, my business manager and editor at Jossey-Bass/Pfeiffer, supported the original idea for the book and then made my words good enough to print. Collegial support from the International Society for Performance Improvement (ISPI) and the Institute for Research on Learning (IRL) was much appreciated. And, as usual, my family—Dick, Raye, and Bonnijill—were there with love and patience when I went into my writer's cocoon.

To Sueann Ambron
who always thinks about learning and technology
in the right order

THE AUTHOR

Valorie Beer is director of learning and development at E*TRADE Group. She earned her B.A. degree (1979) in Anthropology at The George Washington University, Washington D.C., and both her M.S.Ed. degree (1981) and Ph.D. degree (1985) in education (curriculum and instruction) at the University of Southern California in Los Angeles. Before joining E*TRADE, she held various technical and management training and organization development positions at Xerox, Western Digital, Apple Computer, and Netscape Communications.

Dr. Beer's main professional activities have focused on the thoughtful use of technology in support of educational goals and workplace productivity. She has published numerous articles on education in nonschool settings, educational evaluation, and strategies for organization development. She is the coauthor (with Clay Carr) of *Personal Job Power* (Peterson's, 1996).

Dr. Beer is a frequent workshop presenter and keynote speaker at professional and academic conferences in the training, educational technology, and organization development fields. She has served as an Advocate of the International Society for Performance Improvement and is an Affiliate Research Scientist at the Institute for Research on Learning.

PART ONE

THE WORLD WIDE WEB'S ROLE IN LEARNING

CHAPTER ONE

WHY WEB LEARNING?

OBJECTIVES

After completing this chapter you will be able to

- Explain current developments about the Web and its use for learning.
- Describe in general terms the contribution that the Web can make to learning environments.

Some History About the Growth of the Web as a Learning Environment

So, how big is the Web as a potential educational resource? Is it just a passing technology fad, another expensive training platform that you will need to replace in a few years?

First, we should step back and recall how much corporations in the United States spend on training—$50 billion per year (Manasco, 1996). Against that, the projections for Web-based training do indeed seem small: Hall (1997) estimated that Web-based training will be a $1.5 billion industry in 2000, or just 3 percent of corporate training expenditures.

However, Web learning, like the Web itself, literally exploded out of nowhere in just a few years. The following statistics illustrate the phenomenal growth of the Web:

- In January 1996 there were 75,000 Web hosts (servers). A year later, there were 408,382 (Semilof, 1997).
- The sale of Web-based training grew 80 percent from 1995 to 1996, and another 150 percent in 1997. Web-based training for Information Technology professionals alone amounted to $92 million in 1996, with a projection of $1.7 billion in 2000 (McKegney, 1997).
- The sale of Web-based curriculum for K–12 schools is experiencing a yearly growth rate of almost 20 percent (Report: Sales, 1997).
- Users of technical training materials predict that in the year 2000 the Web will be a more important training delivery vehicle than static computer-based training (that is, CD-ROM) or electronic performance support systems (Bassi, Cheney, and Van Buren, 1997).

In reality, the Web is not everywhere, and many of your learners will not have access to it, a factor you will consider in Chapter Three. However, the statistics show that the Web is here to stay, and can therefore be considered as a potent tool for learning. The following sections explain why.

Why the Web Is Important to Learning

"The harsh reality for the 21st century is that if you don't have access to PCs and the Internet, you won't participate in communication, education, entertainment and commerce" (Einstein, 1998, quoting Mark Benioff, senior vice president at Oracle). Benioff's comment is both a warning and a call to action for educators. The growing presence of the Web, and the central role it has taken in information access and dissemination, means that you can spend less time searching for information and more time creating meaning. This also means that learners can have the most up-to-date information and can more easily access and engage the experts who create that information.

Unfortunately, this does not mean that the Web will create knowledge or learning any faster or more easily or less expensively than any other educational vehicle. If we think of the Web as the latest educational medium, rather than just the media container that it is, we will end up repeating the history we had with television or computers in the classroom. We might once again begin to hope that a medium will solve our educational problems—even if we don't bother with thorough audience analysis and solid instructional design.

Therefore, the best way to think about the Web for learning is not how to use it to replace your classroom instructors. A better approach is to add the Web to the learning environment that your company already has that may include classrooms, self-study, computer-based training, mentoring, and other educational strategies. Rather than trying to re-create other learning venues in the Web, the best way to use the Web for learning is to take advantage of what it is uniquely good for:

- Providing learning that does not need to happen at a particular place or time, but that does require the most up-to-date information (such as how to use a new product, or how to respond to a competitor's latest move)
- Providing learning environments that can be configured by the learners for their own needs and learning styles (by using bookmarks, or by creating their own links to useful material)
- Giving classroom instructors the latest information so that they spend time helping learners rather than being taken out of the classroom for "refresher" training
- Enabling synchronous or asynchronous collaboration and conversation between instructors, learners, and experts who are distant from each other in time or space
- Providing refresher training or shortcuts for more experienced learners who already know how to use the Web and who can find what they are looking for on it
- Giving learners the ability to contribute (publish) directly to the learning environment so that others can benefit immediately from information they have found, procedures they have used successfully, and problems they have encountered and solved
- Providing instructional designers with an open-standards environment that allows them to focus on learning rather than spending large amounts of time converting training modules to a plethora of file formats for different computer platforms

EXHIBIT 1.1. WHAT THE WEB IS GOOD FOR (AND NOT GOOD FOR) IN LEARNING ENVIRONMENTS.

The Web is good for learning environments that:

- Do not need to happen at a particular place or time

- Require the most up-to-date information

- Encourage learners to arrange the content for their own needs and learning styles.

- Have constantly changing information that classroom instructors need to know about

- Encourage collaboration and conversation between instructors, learners, and experts

- Provide refresher training or shortcuts for experienced learners

- Encourage learners to contribute (publish) their own material to the learning environment

- Contain a variety of computer hardware and software platforms

The Web is not good for learning environments that:

- Provide just-in-time training to learners who may not have access to a computer when they need it

- Involve novice computer users who may need to learn to use the Web first

- Have materials that were originally designed for another medium (without first reworking them for the Web)

You also need to consider what the Web is not good for, so that you will not waste your resources in that direction. The Web is not useful as just another self-paced, allegedly just-in-time learning platform. Other self-paced learning platforms (such as CDs) are easier to focus on a particular content area. And just-in-time implies that your learners know where to find the information they need, which can be a difficult task for novices on the information-laden Web. The Web also is not useful as an on-line repository for the electronic version of the student manual or instructor guide from a classroom course. There was a reason that you chose classroom instruction for the original course, and putting the classroom materials on a Web site loses the instructor guidance and peer interaction that may have been an important part of the class.

FAST-GLANCE SUMMARY

Exhibit 1.1 summarizes what the Web is good for, and not good for, in learning environments. This will help you makes some preliminary decisions about using the Web. The tools in Chapter Three will help you make a more detailed assessment.

To Learn More About . . .

The market for Web-based training:

Hall, B. (1997). *Web-based training: Market trends, risks, and opportunities.* Sunnyvale, CA: Multimedia & Internet Training Newsletter.

CHAPTER TWO

HOW THE WEB IS USED FOR LEARNING

OBJECTIVES

After reading this chapter, you will be able to
- List the ways in which the Web is used to support learning.
- Describe some of the characteristics that you want your Web learning environment to have, based on your analysis of sites listed in this chapter.
- Explain some of the pitfalls that you want to make sure to avoid in your Web learning environment.

How to Use This Chapter

This chapter is for browsing and searching and seeing what you like (and do not like) about Web sites that claim to be educational. This chapter explains how the Web is currently used as an environment for learning. Information, guidelines, and tools for determining if and how you should use the Web for learning are the subject of the rest of this book.

Learn About the Web on the Web

You will want to read this chapter with a Web browser up and running nearby. The learning sites listed in this chapter (all of which are linked from the book's Web site: http://www.pfeiffer.com/beer.html) do not require registration for you to access some or all of the site. In addition, most of the sites have complete or demonstration learning modules that you can try for free. Although most of the sites pertain to workplace learning, a few university and K–12 sites are listed because they are great examples of how the Web can be used for learning. In these sites you can ignore the specific content, which tends to be mostly about math and science for kids, and pay attention to how the sites structure and present content and learning activities and how they organize resources for instructors.

Of course, the lists in this chapter are not all-inclusive; Web sites change daily. In addition, there are many more good examples of Web learning sites that are behind company firewalls or that require payment or registration. At the companion Web site to this book, you are invited to recommend other good learning Web sites that you may come across or that you have built.

How to Look at the Web Sites in this Chapter

The purpose of this chapter is for you to get some ideas about what works, and what does not, in educational Web sites before you build your own. Rosenfeld and Morville (1998) recommend two simple questions that you can use to begin your assessment of the sites in this chapter:

- What did you hate about the site?
- What did you like about the site?

As Rosenfeld and Morville point out, it is important to answer the "hate" question, because you are most likely to notice first (and remember longest) what got in your way and made the site hard to use. These are the same things that may prevent your learners from learning anything at your Web site.

Here are some additional questions to consider:

- What did you learn at this Web site (other than that you liked or hated it)?
- Can you do something now that you could not do before (that is, did you learn a new skill)?
- If so, what was it about the Web site that enabled you to learn? Was it the way the content was arranged? the exercises that you did? the person you chatted with or e-mailed from the Web site?

EXHIBIT 2.1. QUESTIONS TO ASK ABOUT WEB LEARNING SITES.

1. What did I hate about the site?

2. What did I like about the site?

3. What did I learn at this Web site (other than that I liked or hated it)?

4. Can I do something now that I could not do before (that is, did I learn a new skill)?

5. If so, what was it about the Web site that enabled me to learn? Was it the way the content was arranged, the exercises that I did, the person that I chatted with or e-mailed from the Web site?

6. If I did not learn anything from the site, why not? What got in the way of my learning?

- If you did not learn anything from the site, why not? What got in the way of your learning?

    Try to be as specific as possible in noting what it was about the Web site that caused you to learn, or kept you from learning. You will want to include the successful strategies—and avoid the others—as you build your own Web learning environment.

    Exhibit 2.1 lists these questions in a form that you can copy and have with you as you review learning Web sites.

Where to Start

There are hundreds of public Web sites that purport to have learning as their goal. A good place to start is with sites that review Web learning sites and other Web learning resources. These will help you to narrow the list of sites you want to visit.

Web-Based Training Information Center
http://www.Webbasedtraining.com

Tom Kiley's comprehensive and long-running (in Web years) site lists (but generally does not evaluate) over 200 educational Web sites. The site also includes how-tos and guidelines for creating Web-based training, extensive lists of resources and tools, and a discussion area for sharing your ideas and questions with other Web educators.

Pacific Bell's Knowledge Network Explorer
http://www.kn.pacbell.com/wired/bluewebn

In addition to a list of "Blue Ribbon" Web learning sites, this site contains tutorials, learner activities and projects, lesson plans, resources, references, and tools.

Best Education Sites Today
http://www.education-world.com

This site reviews educational books and Web sites, and provides lesson plans and Web learning project descriptions.

Brian's Educational Web sites
http://home.cwix.com/~b.wasson@cwix.com

This site contains Brian's picks for the top ten educational sites, as well as listing a Site of the Week.

How the Web Is Used for Learning

Web sites that have an educational purpose can be classified into five major groups: mega-sites, catalog sites, delivery sites, resource centers, and tools sites. Four of the types are defined in the upcoming sections, with several examples of each type. (Tools sites are covered in Appendix A.) Because you are most likely using this book to create your own Web learning delivery site, the largest number of examples pertain to this type of site.

Mega-Sites

Mega-sites are like all the other site types combined; they contain course catalogs, resources, and tools, as well as courses that you can take in your Web browser right from the site. The good news about mega-sites is that they have one-stop shopping for almost anything you might need for Web learning. The bad news is that the advertising on these sites often takes up more space (and download time) than the learning modules. In addition, it is easy to get lost in the huge shopping and learning mall-type environment that is typical of these sites.

Mega-sites are important to look at if you will be creating and managing a large Web learning environment with many educational resources.

Here are some examples of mega-sites for Web learning:

Maricopa Center for Learning and Instruction (hundreds of links to Web learning examples)
http://www.mcli.dist.maricopa.edu

Training Magazine (courses, publications, software, and resources)
http://www.trainingsupersite.com

Catalog Sites

These sites contain lists of learning modules, courses, and other resources, usually with a mix of Web learning and other media types. These sites are an index of what is available for Web learning, and you get the learning either by following the links or by ordering the materials. The good news about catalog sites is that they often have hundreds of offerings, many of which are targeted at international audiences. The bad news is that you're apt to encounter more links that do not work on catalog sites than on any other type of educational site, as the catalog creator often does not have control over the destination links.

Catalog sites are important to look at if you will be indexing the educational offerings from a variety of sources in your company. Many catalog sites are, of course, also delivery sites. The following examples are of sites that are primarily catalogs of educational materials that you then access or purchase elsewhere:

Arragon (huge catalog of continuing education and degree programs)
http://www.arragon.com

Ascolta Training Company (catalog of classroom-delivered Information Technology courses and certification providers)

http://www.ascolta.com

California Virtual University (catalog of distributed learning programs offered by California colleges and universities)
http://www.virtualu.ca.gov

Cambridge Center for Adult Education (catalog of classroom-delivered continuing education courses; a few Web-delivered courses are also listed)
http://www.ccae.org

Learning Solutions Alliance (catalog of classroom-delivered courses)
http://www.learningsolutions.com

Motorola University (corporate training catalog)
http://www.mu.motorola.com

New Promise (searchable index of on-line college courses; also contains
articles on distributed learning)
http://www.caso.com

Virtual University Enterprises (catalog of classroom-delivered Information
Technology courses and certification providers)
http://www.vue.com

World Lecture Hall (links to university-based Web courses worldwide)
http://www.utexas.edu/world/lecture/index.html

Delivery Sites

Delivery sites provide all sorts of learning environments, including
- Pages of static content (on-line books)
- Multimedia presentations
- Guided tours
- Animations and simulations
- Tests, surveys, and other forms of assessment
- Asynchronous interactions with other learners and instructors through
  e-mail and discussion boards
- Classroom-like synchronous environments with shared whiteboards and
  notes spaces, conferencing and small group capabilities, polling, and the
  option for learners to "raise their hand" to ask questions or give input

The good news about delivery sites is that there are a plethora of them out there; you can learn almost anything on the Web, and have contact with experts, educators, and other learners to an extent that was not previously possible.

The bad news about delivery sites falls in several areas that you will want to avoid in building your own Web learning environment:

—There is very little practice and assessment on any of these sites that would enable learners to try out new skills and prove that they have learned them.

—On many sites the only "learning" activity is clicking the mouse.

—Few sites do a good job of chunking the content to take into account screen sizes and navigation limitations.

—Multimedia components and simulations often require special software and considerable computer memory.

—Most discussions in asynchronous environments are off-topic and poorly moderated.

—Synchronous classroom-like environments fail to scale well when classes get too large or cross too many time zones.

Since you are using this book to build Web learning environments, the sites listed in this section deserve a careful review so that you will have an idea of what to do—and what not to do—in your own sites. Remember the "reality check questions" as you review these sites.

Web Learning Reality Check!

- Do you learn this way?
- Do you know anyone who does?
- Could you learn what you are expecting others to learn from your Web site?

ℛ ℛ ℛ ℛ ℛ ℛ

Here are a few examples of the many sites that deliver primarily self-paced learning:

Computerworld's Quickstudy Sub-site (wraps each piece of content in a "context story" that helps the learner see the larger picture; also provides definitions, related links, and places to go for more information)
http://www.computerworld.com

Hotwired (on-line version of *Wired* magazine; a good example of content chunking that takes into account screen size and navigation; learners practice HTML programming and see the results in side-by-side panels)
http://www.hotwired.com/Webmonkey/html/teachingtool/

Internet Free College (Information Technology courses)
http://www.aavstudio.com/ifc

Pan Media (task-based learning with helpful graphics; does not require plug-ins)
http://www.learn2.com

PBS's Nova Program on the Pyramids (good example of the Guided Tour metaphor; also allows learners to choose how they want to learn and provides a good example of the use of pictures and maps for navigation)
http://www.pbs.org/wgbh/pages/nova/pyramid

Virtual Online University Services' Athena University (international degree and K–12 programs via the Web and e-mail; presentation is primarily text)
http://www.athena.edu/VOU-Home.html

The following are examples of sites that provide instructors, as well as learners, the opportunity to interact asynchronously through e-mail or discussions:

Golden Gate University's CyberCampus (asynchronous instructor-led degree and certificate programs using Web conferencing, telephone, and fax; tests are paper-based and must be taken in a supervised environment, such as a library)
http://cybercampus.ggu.edu

ZD University (self-paced or asynchronous instructor-led training on computer applications, with hands-on practice but no assessment; also

includes message boards, a virtual café, resources, and instructor office hours; payment is by time spent on the site, not by course)
http://www.zdu.com

Asynchronous Learning Networks (an organization devoted to the subject, with a site offering journals, products, research, and workshops)
http://www.aln.org

Two additional sites provide synchronous, classroom-like learning environments:

Interactive Learning International Corporation (attempts to replicate the classroom environment as closely as possible, providing synchronous learning experiences)
http://www.ilinc.com

Language Connect (Spanish language instruction using a synchronous Web environment resembling a physical classroom as well as other media)
http://www.languageconnect.com/Institute/index.html

One site that does not fit neatly into the categories described thus far, but that is worth a visit just to experience its unique approach, is *Western Governors' University* (**http://www.wgu.edu**). WGU is an attempt to provide a "campus-less" competency-based learning environment that includes the Web, computer-based training, print materials, television, video and audio tapes, voice mail, videoconferencing, and satellite broadcast.

Resource Centers

These sites contain research results, policy statements, conference proceedings, case studies, and guidance on Web learning. You probably will not point your learners to these sites, but they will be valuable for your own reference as you build your Web learning environments. The good news about resource sites is that the case studies and discussions, in particular, can give you a reality check on what it takes to build and maintain a Web learning environment. The bad news about these sites is that a sales pitch for the site's products is often disguised as research or examples. A few of the best K–12 and higher education Web resource sites are listed at the end of this section.

They are worth a look because their research and examples usually come without a sales pitch.

The following sites are good resources for how to use technology for workplace learning in general, and how to do instructional and technical design for Web learning environments in particular:

Association for the Advancement of Computing in Education (catalog site of journals on the uses of technology in learning)
http://www.aace.org/pubs

Bovik Research (demonstration projects on how technology is being used for learning)
http://www.bovik.org

Brandon Hall Resources (guidelines and articles on how to use the Web for learning)
http://www.brandon-hall.com

Cognitive Arts (formerly the Institute for Learning Sciences; research and projects on the educational uses of interactive simulations, artificial intelligence, and cognitive psychology)
http://www.lscorp.com

EdWeb (guidelines and case studies on how to use the Web for learning)
http://edweb.gsn.org

EPSS.COM (articles, conferences, case studies, and presentations on electronic performance support systems; contains a growing Web-based performance support component)
http://www.epss.com

Instructional Management Systems (technical standards for Web-based education)
http://www.imsproject.org

SRI's Center for Technology Learning (research on uses of technology in education)
http://www.sri.com/policy/ctl

Utah State University, School of Education, Department of Instructional Technology (articles on instructional design research, including theory-based technology tools for creating learning environments)
http://www.coe.usu.edu/it/id2

The following are a few of the many resource sites that address Web learning from a K–12 or higher education perspective:

Alberta Education, Province of Alberta, Canada (good example of a Web site for education stakeholders; site has bilingual versions)
http://ednet.edc.gov.ab.ca

EDUCAUSE (policy papers, demonstration projects, and publications on using information technology in higher education)
http://www.educause.edu

Genentech's Access Excellence (the best-organized educational resource site; a good model regardless of what and who you are teaching)
http://www.gene.com/ae/

University of Minnesota College of Education and Human Development (how to use the Web for learning; e-mail discussion groups for educators who are using the Web; technology resource center)
http://web66.coled.umn.edu

FAST-GLANCE SUMMARY

- You can jump-start the design of your own Web learning site by analyzing what works—and what does not work—in existing educational Web sites.
- There are five major categories of Web sites that support learning:
  Mega-sites that provide courses, tools, articles, and access to experts and colleagues.
  Catalog sites that list educational resources that are available over the Web and through other media.
  Delivery sites that deliver self-paced or instructor-led content, learning activities, and assessments. These sites may also include training management elements such as registration, learner tracking, course scheduling, and payment.

Resource sites that contain education policy and research papers and discussions with educators.

Tools sites that contain software packages, templates, and code for building your own Web learning environment. (Tools sites are listed in Appendix A.)

To Learn More About . . .

Companies that provide Web learning products:

Hall, B. (1997). *Web-based training: Market trends, risks, and opportunities.* Sunnyvale, CA: Multimedia & Internet Training Newsletter.

McKegney, M. (1997, Sept. 8). Training via Nets starts to heat up. *Web Week*, pp. 17–18.

How to evaluate computer-based training:

Hall, B., & Sprenger, P. (1997, July). Team training. *Internet World*, pp. 58–60.

Sites that deliver synchronous and asynchronous Web-based training (includes a list and evaluation of sites):

Driscoll, M. (1998). *Web-based training.* San Francisco: Jossey-Bass/Pfeiffer, chapter 8.

PART TWO

PREPARING TO USE
THE WEB FOR LEARNING

The two introductory chapters that you just read described the growth and current uses of the Web for workplace teaching and learning. You may have already made the decision (or been given a mandate) to use the Web as a vehicle for learning in your workplace. However, before you begin creating your Web learning environment, you will want to assess how your learners are likely to accept and use Web technology, and then make your case for the most effective use of Web learning in your company.

The three chapters in this section will help you do that. First, you will find tools and ideas for conducting an assessment to determine how, and if, the Web will be used by your learners. The second chapter in the section describes the critical importance of human-to-human (and not just human-to-computer) interaction in learning, and why the Web is well suited to creating communities of learners. Finally, some of the major strengths and drawbacks of the Web for learning will be presented.

Like all technologies, the Web has advantages and limitations, and using it for real learning projects is often harder than you might have imagined (or at least different). It is true that the Web, unlike many other educational technologies, "may be the ideal tool to nurture students' willingness to take risks, commitment to talk, curiosity, openness to experience, broad interests, originality, imaginative play, intuition, attraction to novelty and complexity, artistic ability, metaphorical thinking, problem finding, elaboration of ideas, and breaking away from the norm" (Bonk and Reynolds, 1997, pp. 168–169). But this does not mean that your employees will automatically learn anything from it, or that they will use it to interact or collaborate any more than they already do.

The ideas and tools in this section will help you to set the stage for making sure that the Web will work in your learning environment. At the end of the section, you will find a presentation outline that will help you bring together all the ideas presented so far in the book to make a strong case for how the Web should be used for learning in your company.

CHAPTER THREE

LEARNING ENVIRONMENTS

OBJECTIVES

After reading this chapter, you will be able to
- Determine if the Web is appropriate for what you need to teach.
- Assess whether or not Web technology and Web learning will be compatible with your workplace environment and acceptable to your learners.

Analyzing the Workplace Environment

Why is it important to analyze your learners' workplace before you build a Web learning environment for them? Why not just follow the trend and make all training Web-based?

This chapter is designed to help you avoid the trap of putting learning on the Web just because the technology is exciting and bursting with possibilities. Even if you have already chosen to put part of your company's learning environment on the Web, you still need to find out how your learners expect and prefer to learn. While it is true that the Web does seem to be everywhere, the Web probably is not the actual workplace for most of your employees. Unless your learners are programmers, network engineers, or Webmasters, whatever they learn on the Web will not be in the context of what they do every day at work. For most of us, Web learning, like classroom training, is not situated in the real work environment, because our work environment is not the Web or the classroom.

The Learner-Technology Assessment

To make sure that the Web will be accepted and used as a learning tool in your workplace, you need to take a look at your learners to see how they currently learn, what tools they use, and what space, both physical and psychological, they have available for Web learning. Therefore, before you start creating a Web learning environment, you will need to conduct a learner-technology assessment (LTA). The LTA is in addition to the needs assessment that you already do to determine what skills your audience needs to learn. The LTA complements the regular needs assessment by focusing on how your learners will accept and use the training delivery technology (in this case, the Web). (Needs assessment resources appear in the "To Learn More About" section at the end of this chapter.)

The LTA will help you answer three critical questions:

- Is the Web appropriate for the content or skills that your audience needs to learn?
- What technology does your audience currently use to learn?
- What is the likely impact on this audience of introducing the Web as a learning tool?

The third question is crucial and often overlooked. Just because your audience already uses the Web in their work environment does not necessarily mean that they will adopt it as a learning tool. Before you go to the expense of creating a Web site, you need to find this out.

Responding to Mandated Moves to the Web

Surprisingly, the LTA will also help you defend against the mandate that training managers frequently hear about putting all of a company's training on the Web. (Perhaps you have been given such a mandate yourself.) It is unlikely that the answer to "How does your audience learn?" will be "By sitting in front of a computer screen for hours and hours." No one in your company learns that way, but you may need data from real employees to prove it. The LTA will give you that data. It will also help you convince your colleagues that there are good reasons

- *For* a multifaceted learning environment (of which the Web may be a part)
- *Against* converting all of your company's classroom or computer-based training to HTML and posting it on a Web site

Together, the needs assessment and learner-technology assessment will help you determine which instructional strategies and media choices will work best for your learners. These assessments will help you find out what your learners need and what their learning environment is like before you rush to the Web (or any other medium). Before you build it, make sure they will use it.

Using the Learner-Technology Assessment Tool

The LTA has two parts that address the first two questions that were raised earlier in the chapter—determining if the Web is an appropriate way to deliver the content, and determining what technology your audience already uses for learning. The data you collect in these two areas will help you answer the third question: whether or not Web learning will be accepted as part of you workplace environment. Exhibit 3.1 shows the learner-technology assessment form.

LTA Part 1: Determining the Suitability of the Web for the Content. In the first part of a learner-technology assessment, you look at what needs to be learned (that is, at the results of your needs assessment) and determine if the Web provides an appropriate environment for addressing the objectives and presenting the content and practice that your learners need. Regardless of the work environment, which could be anything from an aircraft maintenance hangar to a hospital to a sales outlet, you will find five elements in every learning environment: goals, content, presentation of material, practice activities, and assessment.

EXHIBIT 3.1. LEARNER-TECHNOLOGY ASSESSMENT FORM.

Part 1: Determining the Suitability of the Web for the Content

1. Could the Web contribute to meeting the learning goals?
2. Is the Web an appropriate container for the content (that is, the information to be conveyed)?
3. Is the way that the content is presented now amenable to Web presentation?
4. Can the learner gain information and practice new skills on the Web?
5. Can you be reasonably sure that the learners have the new skill, based on what they learned on the Web?

Part 2: Determining the Acceptability of the Web in the Learning Environment

1. How do employees of this company learn now?
2. Who is asking for Web learning, and why?
3. How do you envision employees using a Web learning environment?
4. Do employees know how to use Web technology?
5. Do employees want to learn this way?
6. What key elements of the company's language or culture could be used to help the Web learning environment be accepted?
7. What technology is needed for the Web learning environment, and does it exist in this company?

Five Elements of Learning Environments

Learning Goal

Someone in your company has recognized the need to solve a problem that requires new information and a way to apply it (that is, a new skill).

Example: Sales representatives will be able to give a presentation that compares our company's products with those from the competition.

Content Related to the Goal

This is the information that the employee needs and may or may not know where to find.

Example: Descriptions of products from our company and from our competitors.

Presentation of Content

The information is presented somewhere: in a manual, in a test result, in a conversation with a coworker.

Example: Product brochures produced by our company and by our competitors.

Learning Activity

This is the behavior that an employee engages in to find the content, interact with its presentation, learn the information, and try out the new skill.

Example: Sales representatives prepare a feature-by-feature comparison of one product from our company and a similar product from the competition.

Assessment

Most employees do not give themselves tests; however, they readily apply information and skills to try and solve the problem that caused them to have the learning goal.

Example: Sales managers evaluate the sales representatives' product comparison for completeness and accuracy.

ᔕᖾ ᔕᖾ ᔕᖾ ᔕᖾ ᔕᖾ ᔕᖾ

These five elements characterize a learning environment. To see if a Web learning environment might be appropriate for what your employees need to learn, turn the five characteristics into questions. Use Part 1 of the LTA form to record your data.

Sample Learning Goal and Web Possibilities

Goal: Sales representatives will be able to give a presentation that compares our company's products with those from the competition.

1. *Could the Web contribute to meeting all or part of the learning goal?*
   The Web may be a good source of product information, if both your
   company and the competition have put product descriptions on their
   Web sites. The Web will be less effective in teaching about how to give
   a presentation, as practice in front of a live audience is crucial to be able
   to apply the skill appropriately.
2. *Is the Web an appropriate container for the content?* Because many companies now have Web sites, the content for the product comparisons may
   already be on the Web. Even the content for how to give an effective product demonstration, including a video example, could be put on the Web.
3. *Is the way that the content is presented now amenable to Web presentation?* You could use your own Web learning site to link to the competition's
   site, or to provide side-by-side comparisons of products from different
   companies. Some of the content on presentation skills, such as immediate
   feedback from a presentation coach, would be better in a live setting.
4. *Can the learner gain information and practice new skills on the Web?*
   The sales representatives can get product information from the Web.
   They might practice creating "cheat sheets" that compare products
   from your company and from the competition, and then posting those
   sheets to a Web site or e-mailing them to colleagues for comment. Practicing the product presentation needs to be done with a live audience,
   so the Web is less useful for this part of the goal.
5. *Can you be reasonably sure that the learners have the new skill, based
   on what they learned on the Web?* Sales managers could evaluate the
   "cheat sheets" that learners have posted or e-mailed on the Web. Assessing the sales representatives' presentation skills will need to be done in a
   more real-time, visual medium (such as in a conference room or via
   videoconference).

$$\wp \quad \wp \quad \wp \quad \wp \quad \wp \quad \wp$$

The last question about making sure that your learners can demonstrate their new skills on the Web is crucial. Unless your learners are programmers, network engineers, or Webmasters, their work does not happen on the Web. Therefore, you cannot be assured that they have the new skill until they prove it off the Web, in the real work environment. For many content areas, especially those that involve real-time human interaction (such as presentations) or physical activities (such as repairing machines), there is no way for your learners to use the Web to practice and demonstrate mastery of new skills completely and in context. (However, if your learners do use the Web and computers as part of their everyday work, then the Web is the perfect place for them to practice and demonstrate their competence.)

LTA Part 2: Determining the Acceptability of the Web in the Learning Environment.   If you are going to use the Web to help your learners gain new skills and knowledge, you will need to make sure that the Web learning environment fits into the way employees already learn, at least initially. Even if the Web is currently part of your company's technical infrastructure, it may not be seen as a place to go for learning. If your learners need to leave their work, either physically (such as going to a computer station) or psychologically (such as using the Web for an unfamiliar task), then you will need to know that so you can help them apply their Web-learned skill back on the job.

The second part of the LTA answers the question, Who is learning what, and how are they learning it now? Your company's employees are learning all the time, with or without a formal training program. What you need is to look beyond that program to where work and learning gets done, and ask the question, Will the Web be accepted as a part of our learning environment?

The seven questions in Part 2 of the LTA will help you assess whether or not the Web will be accepted into the way learning happens at your company. You can use surveys, focus groups, interviews, and observation to find out the answers to these questions.

Seven Questions About the Technology That Learners Use

1. *How do employees of this company learn now?* You need to find out how your employees learn their job skills now so you can assess whether the Web will fit with their learning style. This requires more than just looking at the courses offered by the training department; it requires asking or observing what employees do when they need to learn something. Do they
   - Consult a manual?
   - Ask a colleague inside the company?
   - Contact an expert outside of the company?
   - Conduct trial-and-error experiments until they find something that works?
   - Sign up for a class?
   - Do a Web search?

   Finding the answer to how employees learn now tells you much more than whether or not they currently use the Web. The answer tells you what types of interactions you might want to build into your Web learning environment so that it will not be so different from how learning happens already. For example, if employees are accustomed to asking colleagues how to do a task, then you will want to make sure that facilities for doing that (such as chat rooms, discussion boards, or e-mail) are part of the Web learning environment.

   The more your new Web learning feels like the way learning already happens, the more your employees are likely to accept it. Of course, you can expand this once your learners are accustomed to the Web—but to get them started, you should provide them with a familiar way of learning that just happens to employ the Web, rather than trumpeting the Web as "the new way to learn." The Web (or any other technology) will not be embraced by employees if it requires them to learn the technology at the same time that they are trying to learn the content.

2. *Who is asking for Web learning, and why?* Are employees asking for Web-based learning opportunities? Or is the impetus coming from cost-conscious executives who want all training on-line? There are usually two reasons for the latter:

- To eliminate expensive training rooms and instructors
- To enable employees to take training at home on their off-hours

Chapter Five will give you some arguments to make against the proposition that Web learning can eliminate classroom training. For the second Web learning rationale—the separation of learning from work—Ambrosio (1998) has noted, "Increasingly stressed out workers opt or feel they are expected to take work-related training on their own time—at night or on weekends—so that they remain 'productive' during work hours." If this is the reason for moving to Web learning in your company, then you will want to investigate employees' willingness to learn on their own time. In addition, you will need to know about the technical infrastructure (such as secure remote network access and laptop computers with Web browsers and modems) that will enable them to do so via the Web.

3. *How do you envision employees using a Web learning environment?* Computer-based training (CBT) has long been associated with individual, self-paced learning. Is this the tradition of computer-based training at your company? Is this how you envision your company's employees using a Web learning environment? Because of the interactive nature of the Web, and the ability to keep Web content up to date more easily, there are broader learning possibilities than with static CBT. By anticipating how learners will use the Web, you will be more likely to persuade both learners and executives that the expense of Web learning is more than offset by its flexibility in serving a variety of learning and performance needs. You should anticipate how employees will use the Web for individual and collaborative learning, performance support, expert tutoring and advice, and update and refresher training.

4. *Do employees know how to use Web technology?* Employees' knowledge of the Web may be limited. Even if they have Web access, you should determine the extent of learners' Web knowledge and their comfort level. Exhibit 3.2 describes four levels of Web use and understanding that you might find among your learners.

5. *Do employees believe that they can learn this way?* Even if the Web is part of your workplace, you will need to find out if employees want to

use it to learn. Will it fit in with their work style and work flow? Or will Web learning be a separate activity, a disruption? Hanley, Schneebeck, and Zweier (1998, p. 4) have noted that "technology utilization patterns" and "preference for using the technology" are key considerations in determining if a technology will be used for learning. Finally, it is worthwhile to remember that a great many learners learn by marking up paper—by highlighting, underlining, making margin notes, or folding a page corner. It is still easier to mark and find paper-based information than it is to do the same with electronic information. Your Web learning environment probably will need to accommodate printing, even if learners are enthusiastic about a "paperless classroom" (Why Paper, 1998).

6. *What key elements of the company's language or culture could be used to help the Web learning environment be accepted?* To be accepted, a Web learning environment needs to have the look and feel (and perhaps sound) of your company's culture. The organization and jargon of your company will give you important keys to how to design your site and what words (such as button labels) to place on it. For example, if your company prides itself on having a nonhierarchical organization, you will want to have a site information architecture that does not suggest levels. Venn diagrams might be a better way to graphically organize content, rather than pyramids or concentric circles (both of which suggest hierarchy). Company language will suggest, for example, whether you use a label that says "Skill Courses" or one that says "Show Me How."

7. *What technology is needed for the Web learning environment, and does it exist in this company?* Web learning requires a considerable amount of expensive equipment, both on the learners' end and on the containers' end (as well as for the network that connects them). Although the hype may lead you to believe that the Web is accessible from almost any computer, you need to be aware of some drawbacks:
   - Different browsers, and different versions of the same browser, may handle Web technology elements (such as frames or fonts) differently.
   - Display technology can affect what the learner sees (such as fonts and colors).
   - Network connection methods and speeds will determine how long learners will be waiting for text and (especially) graphics to arrive and appear in their Web browser screen.

EXHIBIT 3.2. FOUR LEVELS OF WEB USE BY LEARNERS.

Level of Web Use	Considerations for This Level
1. Learner is new to the Web	You may need to teach them how to use the Web before you use the Web to teach them. These learners will find it difficult to learn a skill while also learning how to use the technology that is teaching them that skill. You will want to make sure the technology itself is not a roadblock to learning and competence.
2. Learner is accustomed to CBT	This group equates computer-based learning with self-paced learning. They may not know how to learn collaboratively. As Butler (1997, p. 422) has noted, these learners may not "have experience as active participants in public 'discussions'; hence, they may not consider issues such as quality, content appropriateness, and intellectual property." In addition, it may not occur to them that they can contact a real person to get help in a computer-based learning environment, which is possible with Web-based chats, discussions, and e-mails.
3. Learner experienced with Web technology	This group probably will know how to learn from the Web, and may go browsing in places you never imagined. This is good if you have given them the capability to link what they find into the Web learning site. This is not good if your site does not easily allow them to find their way back to the learning environment This group may also know so much about Web technology that they are compelled to comment on the information architecture, user interface, and other elements of your site's design, rather than focusing on the learning that they are supposed to get from it. If your audience falls into this category, make sure you provide a "feedback" or "contact us" mechanism.
4. Learner prefers to browse with graphics off	This group knows how to use the Web, but has a preference for text only. Or they may work in an environment such as a remote location with a slow network that makes downloading graphics difficult. Restrictions on graphics will affect both your instructional strategy and your Web site design, so it is important to determine early on if graphics can or will be used by your learners.

♫ ♫ ♫ ♫ ♫ ♫

Developing a Proposal Based on the LTA. You can use the results of your LTA to make a proposal or presentation about what you think your Web learning environment will look like. You can also use the results to make sure that your learners have the technology (both hardware and software) to render the Web learning environment as you intended it. In addition, you will be able to ensure that learners will have access to that technology when they need it to learn. In the field—that is, away from your main offices—computer (and even electricity) access may be a problem; in some international locations, it may not be available at all. Be sure to include internationally based employees in your LTA so that you will know what technology is available to them, and whether or not the Web will fit in their learning environment.

Tips for Conducting the Learner-Technology Assessment

- *Use anthropological methods rather than technical analyses.* Get out into your workplace and see for yourself how employees learn, how they use technology, and how they collaborate with each other to work and learn.
- *Think beyond the computer screen.* Instead of doing your analysis with the aim of getting the entire learning environment into a two-dimensional computer screen, focus on how you might make the Web a part of a three-dimensional learning environment. Take a look at how employees exploit learning platforms (other than computers) that are already in the environment. Imagine, for example, how you might use the space next to the computer as a place for job aids, checklists, or other performance support tools. There tends to be an empty area within about six inches on either side of most computer monitors. What could you put there that would reinforce Web learning? Most Web-based training sees the computer as central, even in "virtual classroom" environments. However, you might think more broadly about the constellation of learning platforms already available in your workplace—of which the computer, and the Web, could be just one part.
- *Use the Web to do the some of the assessment.* This will involve potential learners in the project from the beginning and will get them accustomed to using Web technology before they use it for learning. You can find out

their biases and preferences about the Web before you start building a learning environment with it.

- *Talk with others who have been there.* People who have attempted to bring a new technology (or a new use for an existing technology) into your work environment may have valuable insights that you could apply. The "Lessons from the Field" interview with Sam Shmikler gives you one Web learning designer's perspective on why a learner-technology assessment, in additional to a needs assessment, is critical to the development of your own Web learning environment.

LESSONS FROM THE FIELD

Assessing Your Company's Readiness for Web Learning

Sam Shmikler is president of the Periscope Organization (http://www.periscope-org.com), which designs information for on-line learning. The group specializes in creating distance learning programs for companies and then measuring the learning gains that result. Before founding the Periscope Organization, Shmikler was a senior training manager at Sun Microsystems and Sybase.

K E Y P O I N T S

Shmikler's Key Points About Readiness for Web Learning:

- Make sure that your target audience, and not just the training managers, are ready for Web learning.
- Web learning is a strategic decision for your company, and requires more than one implementation with a small group.
- A major barrier to a successful and sustainable implementation of Web learning is the belief that the skills and systems needed to create, deliver, and use training on the Web are the same as those needed for print-based or classroom training.

Analyzing Your Company's Readiness for Web Learning

Shmikler: I do four separate audits to determine the readiness and sustainability of Web learning, and to find out where the greatest potential early wins are in the organization. These audits answer the following questions:

1. Are the necessary technology and bandwidth requirements in place so that Web learning will work technically?
2. Is there collaboration between Information Systems, Training, Telecommunications, and the functional business groups; that is, are the people who are creating, delivering, and experiencing the learning environment all talking to each other so that implementation can happen?
3. Will the design and development process and the skills of the instructional design staff—which currently produce print and classroom training—support the development of Web-based learning?
4. Is the intended audience psychologically ready to learn this way, and do they have the necessary technical skills?

The typical Web learning development team is composed of a set of task forces, each of which conducts one of the four audits. If the company is not committed to doing all of the audits, that is a sign that Web learning will be a fad and not a sustainable solution at the company.

Advice for Making the Learning-Versus-Technology Argument

Shmikler: First, determine what the real drivers of Web learning are in the company by asking the following questions:

- Is Web learning only going to be used to reduce delivery costs?
- Is it a time-to-market issue for the training programs themselves? That is, will the Web reduce the time it takes to create a course and get it ready to deliver?
- Is it a reach issue? That is, you cannot get to your target audience another way?
- Is it a time-to-volume issue? That is, how long is it going to take you to train every last person in the target audience?
- Is it an interference issue? That is, you want to use the Web so that you do not have to interfere with employees' work by taking them away from the workplace to learn?

- Is it because everyone else is doing Web learning?

Depending on the drivers, you will build a design plan that addresses the real needs of the target audience and includes a companywide, sustainable Web learning strategy. The worst thing a department can do is experiment with Web learning at a tactical "course" level when you have so many strategic and cross-functional groups that you need an effective distributed learning system.

After the drivers, the next major issue is that learning plans last, but technology does not. Most companies need to make their technology decisions based on a one-year plan, but the design of learning needs to be forecast further out. In addition, you need to build a team that can prepare Web learning on a sustained, production basis, not on a one-off, pilot basis. Most companies are not coming to grips with the realization that Web learning requires a reformulation of how they build courses.

The final issue is preparing learners to be effective and efficient Web learners. This "socialization" aspect is tripping up many training departments at this time.

Major Barriers to Implementing Web Learning in the Workplace

Shmikler: There are six major barriers to Web learning:

1. Training departments that want to completely control the delivery system. It may have worked in the past with overhead projectors, but it will not work with the Web.
2. Training developers who spend all of their time playing with the technology rather than coming up with a design model that ensures learning effectiveness.
3. A narrow definition of "interactivity" that is limited to point-and-click and animation.
4. Assuming that Web learning development is subject to the same restrictions imposed by print production for classrooms.
5. Overly controlling the learners in ways that violate their natural and "Web encouraged" love of discovery.
6. Failing to use the digital format of Web learning to facilitate both tutorial (directed learning) and post-learning needs (electronic performance support).

Content and Skills Appropriate for the Web

🖐   **Shmikler:** Good candidates include

- Large-scale software implementations
- Soft skills, such as "customer care" simulations
- Electronic commerce solutions
- Software training
- Manufacturing process changes

Advice for Web Learning Developers

🖐   **Shmikler:**

- Do not overcommit; Web learning development takes time.
- Recognize that your technology platform will change before your pilot project is completed.
- Think in terms of the "shelf-life" of the knowledge, skills, and capabilities, not in terms of the next technology revision.
- Do not jump on the Web learning bandwagon just because one executive (who could be gone before your project is completed) wants it.
- If you do decide to create Web learning environments, focus on creating "production grade" processes that will make Web learning a sustainable solution in your company, and that will outlast the one key evangelist or Web guru who is currently pushing Web learning.

🖐 🖐 🖐 🖐 🖐 🖐

FAST-GLANCE SUMMARY

- Before you design a Web learning environment, you will need to find out how the Web fits into employees' work, and how (or if) they will use it for learning.
- Two tools, the needs assessment and the learner-technology assessment, help you determine what your learners need to learn and if the Web is right for your workplace and for your learners
- The learner-technology assessment helps you determine whether or not The Web is appropriate for what you need to teach.

The Web can provide enough real practice for your learners.

Web learning will be accepted as a vehicle for learning in your company.

- You need to assess your company's readiness for Web learning, to think of it as a strategy and not as just a pilot test of a new technology. This assessment includes making sure that

The technology is in place.

All relevant groups—trainers, systems engineers, and users—are working together to bring the Web learning environment to fruition.

Instructional designers and instructors have the skills to create Web learning.

Employees are ready to use the Web for learning.

To Learn More About ...

Anthropological methods:

Pelto, P. J. (1970). *Anthropological research: The structure of inquiry.* New York: Harper & Row.

Learning needs assessment:

Goldstein, I. L. (1992). *Training in organizations: Needs assessment, development, and evaluation.* Pacific Grove, CA: Brooks/Cole.

Rossett, A. (1987). *Training needs assessment.* Englewood Cliffs, NJ: Educational Technology Publications.

Zemke, R., & Kramlinger, T. (1982). *Figuring things out.* Reading, MA: Addison-Wesley.

Skills assessment software:

Auerbach, S. (1997, July/August). Mining for skills. *Inside Technology Training,* pp. 40–53.

International and cross-cultural learning considerations:

Collins, B., & Remmers, E. (1997). The World Wide Web in education: Issues related to cross-cultural communication and interaction. In B. Khan (Ed.), *Web-based instruction* (pp. 85–92). Englewood Cliffs, NJ: Educational Technology Publications.

Situated learning:

Brown, J. S., Collins, A., & Duguid, P. (1989, January-February). Situated cognition and the culture of learning. *Educational Researcher,* pp. 32–42.

CHAPTER FOUR

𝔰 𝔰 𝔰 𝔰 𝔰 𝔰

COMMUNITIES OF LEARNERS

OBJECTIVES

After reading this chapter you will be able to

- Explain why it is important for learners to be connected to others in their workplace while they learn
- Define "learning community"
- Give examples of how the Web can contribute to learning within the communities that already exist in your company

Material for this chapter is based on the work of the Institute for Research on Learning (IRL). IRL is a national nonprofit center that examines what constitutes successful learning in schools, workplaces, and communities and designs learning strategies, tools, environments, and curricula with these insights as the foundation. IRL does this through interdisciplinary and collaborative research, design, and implementation of strategies for learning that are scalable and sustainable. IRL's researchers represent a diverse array of fields, including education, anthropology, computer science, linguistics, cognitive science, sociology, and psychology. The institute's methodologies emphasize participatory design, ethnography, and the creative use of video and video analysis to help see and understand learning as it happens in the real world in myriad settings.

Learning Is Social

In the last chapter, you took a look at your company's readiness for having part of the learning environment available to employees on the Web. One outcome of your learner-technology assessment probably was that you found out how much employees are already learning on the job in collaborative groups or coaching relationships, with or without a formal training plan. To the members of these groups, they are just "working"—learning is an ongoing but unstated part of their workday.

This chapter uses recent research on the social nature of learning to reinforce why it will be important for you to take advantage of the Web's collaboration and interaction tools.

By definition, a workplace is a place where skills and knowledge are applied. A workplace is also a social place; no one in your company works in isolation. It makes sense, then, that workplace learning is social, because skills and knowledge are learned and applied in an environment of collaboration, coordination, and negotiation. While acquiring information may be an individual task, creation of knowledge is not, as it is from the social context of peers, managers, and customers that your employees get feedback on the correctness and effectiveness of their knowledge and skill.

These points about the social nature of learning will be especially important for you to emphasize with your instructional designers and learners. Using the Web can enhance the group learning that is already occurring in abundance in your company. Yet both groups may be operating from an old model of computer-based training, or an even older model of school-based education. These models say that valid learning occurs only when individuals do their own work, and that collaboration is cheating.

Workplace Competence

Competence in the workplace is not defined by individuals. It is defined by what employees do together as a company (a workplace "community") to please customers and keep the business going. Employees want to participate in the community of the workplace. Demonstrating a willingness to learn "how we do things here" is often a major prerequisite to an employee's being accepted and allowed to participate in the workplace culture. As Henschel (1996, p. 12) has observed, employees do not learn new skills just to have the skills; they "learn in order to enhance their participation in their communities." Henschel concludes that workplace learning, therefore, is not about passing a "substance" (information) from instructor to student. It involves, instead, a social process of creating and sharing meaning and understanding.

For example, you can use a classroom or job aid to teach the rules (the substance) of how to answer the telephone; however, the real skill of dealing with customers on the telephone depends on the community of employees in your company's call center, who work together to create and disseminate the knowledge of how to resolve customers' problems. The real world of the call center provides the reality check for the rules of telephone etiquette.

Thus, although gathering information may be an individual activity, turning that information into useful knowledge and skill is a social activity. It is the social context—such as talking with customers on the telephone—that gives feedback on the appropriateness and usefulness of the information. Therefore, it is in the work group, or work *community*, where your employees are doing most of their learning, as you probably discovered in your assessment in Chapter Three. As Snyder (1997, p. 9) has observed, "learning occurs most effectively within communities that have developed trust, shared understanding of problems, and a language to communicate new and old solutions." Communities have already formed in your workplace, and your Web learning environment can take advantage of them. The remainder of this chapter defines *learning communities* and explains why they can be an effective part of your Web learning environment.

Why Learning Communities Are Important

According to Etienne Wenger, research scientist at the Institute for Research on Learning (cited by Stamps, 1997, p. 38), a learning community includes

- *Language,* including the documents, images, and symbols that employees use to communicate with each other about their work (such as the terminology that sale representatives use to describe various types of customers)
- *Tools* that employees use to get the work done (such as sales call forms, order forms, customer lists)
- *Explicit roles, procedures, and regulations* that define how employees do their work (such as the steps that a sales representative needs to take to fulfill a customer order)
- *Implicit behaviors* and unstated rules of thumb that make the culture of your workplace unique (such as the "unwritten agreement" that your company's sales representatives will not make negative comments about competitors in front of a customer)

In short, a workplace learning community includes all the formal information that might be conveyed in a classroom course, as well as all the social nuances that make that information work on a daily basis. What a learning community provides—and many formalized educational experiences do not—is context, that is, real workplace problems involving real relationships and real reactions in real time. Because the Web is a real-time environment, you can use it to create or enhance the informal shared learning that is already happening in the communities in your workplace.

How the "Communities of Learning" Concept Applies to Web Learning

Based on their groundbreaking investigations of how learning actually occurs in workplaces, the Institute for Research on Learning has formulated seven principles about the social nature of learning (Seven Principles, 1990). These principles can help you make the case for using the Web's collaborative tools (such as discussions and chat) in your learning environment.

Exhibit 4.1 lists each principle and describes how you might apply it in a Web learning environment.

EXHIBIT 4.1. APPLYING
"COMMUNITIES OF LEARNING" TO THE WEB.

Principle	Application for Workplace and Web Learning
Learning is fundamentally social: A matter of changing "identity," not just acquiring "knowledge"	1. Learners are able to get to a real person in your Web learning environment, by e-mail, chat, discussion, or other. 2. Your learners are not separated from their work environment while they are learning with the Web (sending employees off to a learning lab to work alone at a computer takes them out of the context where they can apply their new skills). 3. You have provided activities—which may not involve the web—where learners can discuss and try out their new knowledge and skills with colleagues.
Knowledge is integrated- into the life of communities: sharing values, perspectives, and ways of doing things creates a "community of practice." Communities can form anywhere, formally and informally, virtually and face to face, and you can be a member of many different communities simultaneously.	1. The Web learning environment fits into how your employees really perform, rather than simply housing the on-line version of the manual. 2. Your web learning community mirrors workplace communities already in place. Forcing learners into artificial groupings such as classes does not help them integrate their learning into their real work group. 3. Find out which communities your learners identify with, such as managers, programmers, sales reps, or contractors. This will give you a key to what information they will access, and whose knowledge (such as which instructors or experts) they will consider credible in the Web learning environment.

(continued on next page)

EXHIBIT 4.1. *(continued)*

Principle	Application for Workplace and Web Learning
Learning is an act of membership: the motivation to learn is the desire to participate in a "community of practice."	1. You encourage your learners to share knowledge in the Web learning environment (for example, by posting their work for others to see and comment on). By doing this, learners show that they can contribute to the workplace community. 2. Your Web learning environment fosters membership among Web learners who may never meet face-to-face, but who nevertheless share a workplace community. 3. You have coached your Web instructors on how to help learners participate in the community.
Knowing depends on engagement in practice: people glean knowledge from observations and participation in a variety of situations and activities.	1. Your Web learning environment points learners to practice activities in the real work environment. 2. Instead of creating separate, distilled information Web pages for your learners, try linking to actual company artifacts (such as business plans or competitive analyses) that have already been published on the company intranet. 3. Organize your learning Web site around what your learners need to do to be productive. Do not organize it around the organization chart or product lines of the company.
Engagement is inseparable from empowerment: individuals perceive their identities in terms of their ability to contribute to and affect the life of a community.	1. Your Web learning environment gives learners real work to do. 2. You provide structured, moderated discussions and chats that include company experts and that help learners feel a part of the workplace community.

EXHIBIT 4.1. *(continued)*

Principle	Application for Workplace and Web Learning
	3. Your Web learning environment provides regular feedback, especially for learning communities who never meet face-to-face.
"Failure" to learn is a common result of exclusion from participation: learning requires access and opportunity to contribute.	1. Your Web learners should have contact with more skilled employees and the work that they are doing, either as part of the Web learning experience or outside it.
	2. If employees are to use the Web learning environment only at home or during off-hours, you have provided other non-Web opportunities for immediately applying what they have learned.
	3. You ensure that your Web learning environment does not depend on specific hardware or software platforms that may not be available to all learners.
We already have a society of ifelong learners: people learn what enables them to participate in the "communities of practice" they want to join.	1. Your Web learning environment fits into the way that employees are already learning in informal or unstructured ways on the job, rather than being trumpeted as "the new (and only) way to learn."
	2. Lifelong learning means that the development of your Web learning environment is never "finished" in the same way that a binder or classroom course is completed for production.
	3. Continuous learning does not mean continuous browsing; the anywhere-anytime nature of the Web makes it a perfect tool for continuous learning within your company, as long as you help your learners focus on their learning needs and help them not get frustrated by the chaos of cyberspace.

What to Consider in Creating Communities of Web Learners

Now is the time to begin thinking about creating communities of Web learners in your workplace, as a community perspective will influence the entire design of your Web learning environment. However, to develop that perspective and create sustainable Web learning communities, Wenger (1996, p. 10) suggests that you be prepared to dispel four myths that others in your company may have about learning:

- Learning is an individual process.
- Learning is separate from other workplace activities, and is not "work."
- Learning has a beginning and an end.
- Teachers are required because learners do not have anything substantive to contribute.

These myths are well ingrained in us by our experiences in school. The first three myths are also characteristic of the design of most computer-based training courses. Therefore, your learners may approach Web learning like they did CD-ROM training: alone in their cubicles, and perhaps in their off-hours so that they cannot be accused of being "unproductive." If you do not overcome the CBT, CD-ROM model of learning as an individual and self-paced activity, you will underutilize the Web and short-change the collaborative learning that chat, discussion, e-mail, real-time publishing, and access to experts make possible.

If you incorporate the Web's collaborative tools in your learning environment, "training becomes not just a matter of designing courses but of facilitating participation" (Wenger, 1996, p. 25). However, to fully take advantage of the community aspects of the Web, using the tools will not be enough. The entire design of your Web learning environment will need to reflect the counterarguments to the four myths shown in Exhibit 4.2.

These ideas about the importance of building collaboration and community among learners are not just some new fad in educational theory; they have already been shown to have a direct impact on the effectiveness of Web learning environments. Hiltz (1995, p. 6) found in her research that "the greatest determinant of the extent to which students feel that the on-line

EXHIBIT 4.2. MYTHS AND REALITIES OF WORKPLACE LEARNING.

The Myth	The Reality
Learning is an individual process.	Learning happens when employees work together to solve business problems.
Learning is separate from other work-place activities, and is not "work."	Learning happens as a natural part of work, and cannot be separated from it.
Learning has a beginning and an end.	Learning happens all the time as employees add to their skills and knowledge so that they can more fully participate in the company's community.
Teachers are required because learners do not have anything substantive to contribute.	Teachers facilitate learning and help learners create knowledge that can contribbute to employee competence.

mode of delivery is better or worse than traditional modes is the amount and quality of interaction between the instructor and the students, and/or among the students."

How to Include "Community" in Your Web Learning Environment

Exhibit 4.3 gives four examples of how you might create Web learning communities. You can delete the examples from this form and use it as a planning tool to ensure that you have built in some collaborative learning in your Web environment.

A Caution About Web Learning Communities

Beware of expecting too much community-building at first on your Web learning site. Your learners may know how to use computers and the Web, but may not have used its collaborative features (such as discussion or chat).

EXHIBIT 4.3. IDEAS FOR BUILDING A WEB LEARNING COMMUNITY.

Community Builders	Ideas for Practice or Assessment
Collaborative projects	Novice sales representatives from across the country create a sales plan for a customer, post it to the Web, and annotate it with their comments on-line.
Tutoring and mentoring of novices by experts	A regional sales manager accesses the sales plan on the Web and coaches the learners on how they might improve the plan.
Community evaluation of work products or projects	A group of sales managers evaluates the sales plan by annotating or sending e-mail about the plan.
Moderated discussions of different perspectives on, and solutions for, a workplace problem	Learners and experienced sales representatives participate in a real-time Web-based chat on how to create a sales plan for a particularly difficult (but desirable) customer.
(Add your ideas here)	

Start by using the Web to enhance the working and learning communities that already exist in your company. Learning how to learn collaboratively on-line may be difficult, especially for learners who are accustomed to the self-paced model of computer-based training. "The Web and the Internet can facilitate collaboration, but they don't create it" (Stamps, 1997, p. 40, quoting Hillen). However, the Web can significantly contribute to information sharing and organizational learning. You can use the Web's collaborative tools to capture, document, and share the knowledge and skills that give your company its competitive edge, so that they will not disappear when employees leave the company.

Chapter Eight will provide you with specific strategies for creating collaborative activities in your Web learning environment.

FAST-GLANCE SUMMARY

- Learning is a social activity. It goes on all the time in your company, with or without a formal training plan or department.
- Competence in the workplace is defined by what employees do together as a company—a *community*—to please customers and keep the business going. Employees work and learn in communities within your company.
- Learning is not about transferring a "substance" (information) from instructors to students; it is about creating a shared set of meanings and skills so that the company can move forward as a whole.
- A learning community includes formal instruction plus the rich context of real problems, solutions, and relationships within which work gets done.
- The individualized nature of school, and the self-paced nature of traditional computer-based training, may make it difficult for your learners to initially accept and use the community tools (such as chat and discussions) that the Web provides.

To Learn More About . . .

Academic and workplace research on learning communities and the social nature of Web learning:

Cognitive Arts (formerly the Institute for Learning Sciences)—
    http://www.lscorp.com.
Institute for Research on Learning—http://www.irl.org.

CHAPTER FIVE

PROS AND CONS OF USING THE WEB FOR LEARNING

OBJECTIVES

After reading this chapter, you will be able to

- Describe seven ways in which the Web helps educators, learners, and business decision makers.
- Explain seven drawbacks to using the Web for learning, and give examples of solutions for overcoming them.
- Use the pros and cons of Web learning, plus the information from previous chapters, to prepare a presentation to your colleagues or management about using the Web for learning in your workplace.

Web Learning: Pros and Cons

Now that you have assessed your learners' work environment and thought about some ways to encourage a learning community through the Web, you are almost ready to begin creating your Web learning environment. However, before you start, you might want to get ready to respond to some of the preconceptions and arguments that your colleagues or your management might have about using the Web for learning. This chapter takes a look at seven aspects of Web learning and the good and bad implications of each. For each "con," some solutions are suggested.

For each of the aspects presented in this chapter, use the "Web Learning Pros and Cons Worksheet" (Exhibit 5.1) to answer some questions about how the pros and cons may apply to your environment. At the end of the chapter, you can use the template provided to put all the information from this and the preceding chapters together into a presentation to make your case for (or perhaps against) using the Web for learning in your company.

Pro #1: Easy Access to Information

You can use the Web to find out something about almost anything with very little effort. Using the Web, your learners will have access to an unprecedented amount of information, assistance, and even real people. You will be able to provide learners with updated information almost instantly. You also only need to maintain the learning materials in one place, the Web server, rather than having to re-master and distribute static media such as paper or CD-ROMs.

For example, you can inform service technicians worldwide that their training Web site now contains an important new learning module on how to fix a particular product. They can access the site at their convenience, quickly learn what the fix is and how to do it, and apply the change immediately to customers' equipment. They can also follow some "Related Links" that you have provided on the site to access the company's press release about the fix, to learn how this fix might affect other products, or to see what is new from the competition. With a wealth of related information just a mouse click away, your service technicians will have a broader context about the equipment and customers they are serving.

Con #1: Information Overload

The problem is that your audience may have too much information. Or they may get lost in cyberspace after the first couple of links. While accessing information is easy on the Web, sifting and sorting it and then creating knowledge from it (that is, figuring out what and how to learn from it) is not so easy. As Duchastel (1997, p. 181) has observed, the Web is "an information-rich but process-poor learning resource."

Just following the links and getting back home is not the only problem that will confront your learners. Suppose that you ask them to do a search

EXHIBIT 5.1. WEB LEARNING PROS AND CONS WORKSHEET.

Pros and Cons of Using the Web for Learning	Questions for Your Learning Environment
Easy Access to Information *versus* Information Overload	1. Is the information that the learners need already on the Web, or will I need to put it there? 2. If the information is already there, will the novice learner be able to make sense of it, or do I need to provide a structure (such as a home page)?
New Ways to Collaborate *versus* Web Collaboration is a New Skill	1. What experience do the learners already have with true Web collaboration (that is, getting work done), and not just with on-line discussions and chat? 2. Which experts or senior managers might I include in the Web collaboration to make it seem more real?
Better Use of Instructors *versus* Instructors Unfamiliar with the Web	1. How are the company's instructors using the Web now? 2. What ideas do the instructors have for good ways to use the Web for teaching?
Maximize Media Capability *versus* Media Overload	1. What (non-Web) media do learners use now? Do they really use video and audio tapes, or is it mostly paper? 2. If I need to teach a skill that seems to require lots of media, is the Web really my best delivery choice?
The Web Seems Ubiquitous *versus* Ubiquitous for Only a Few	1. Does my audience have access to the Web now? 2. How likely is it that my audience will think about going to the Web to learn something?
Web Technologies Run on Many Types of Computers *versus* Many Web Technologies Require Programming Skill	1. Does the training department have the necessary technical skills to create a Web learning environment? 2. If not, can I borrow the expertise from another department, or can I buy it?

(continued on next page)

EXHIBIT 5.1. *(continued)*

Pros and Cons of Using the Web for Learning	Questions for Your Learning Environment
The Web Lowers Learning Costs *versus* The Web Raises Development Costs	1. What will my company save in travel, classroom, or equipment costs if we use the Web for learning? 2. Does the company already have the media producers and programmers to develop the Web learning environment, or will we need to buy the expertise and hardware?

to learn more about a particular topic. Web searches can return thousands of responses, and making sense of the glut can be difficult. Your learners get plenty of information but no clues on how to turn it into knowledge or action—no way to tell how they should go about evaluating the importance, relevance, or accuracy of the data.

For instance, a growing problem with Web information is that it is perceived as true, especially in the medical and health fields, even though the Web is no more immune to quackery and false advertising than any other medium. A well-designed Web site, like one of those infomercials that look like scientific documentaries, can have the convincing appearance of Truth.

Solutions to Information Overload

Do not give Web novices the URL to your learning site and expect them to make efficient use of it as a learning tool on their own. "The consensus is that the Internet model works very well for people who already have considerable expertise in the subject they're researching, but not so well for people who don't" (Gordon, 1997, p. 33). Give your novices some training in how to use Web technology first, and then give them a model (such as an introductory lesson or a guided tour) that shows them what to do and where to click before they have to do it on their own.

At every level on your learning Web site, provide guidance for learners on how to

- Use the information you put there.
- Search—and make sense of search results.
- Know both where they are and how to get back to the preceding page, to the home page of the site, or out of the site entirely.
- Determine if the information they find on other sites is correct and relevant to what they are learning.

Pro #2: New Ways to Collaborate

As you saw in Chapter Two, the Web is a useful vehicle for synchronous and asynchronous collaboration and interaction among learners. The importance of time zones, distance, organizational hierarchies, and status differences among participants (such as novice and expert, young and old, CEO and new-hire) diminish greatly. A Web page on a particular topic, published by one of your company's recognized experts and accompanied by Web e-mail discussion or chat, gives learners direct access to a person who may be able to teach them not only the skill but also the peculiarities of "how we do it here."

In addition, learners can gradually become part of the community of experts by sharing what they find, what they learn, and what new knowledge they create by publishing it on the Web site. As you saw in Chapter Four, small group interaction is crucial to helping your learners develop critical thinking, knowledge, and skills. Using the collaborative tools of the Web, your learners can make direct, real-time contributions to your company's organizational learning, even while they are students taking the Web-equivalent of a class. They do not have to wait until they graduate or are certified to begin sharing information with colleagues and contributing to the company's knowledge base.

Con #2: Web Collaboration is a New Skill

The drawback is that, just because learners have Web collaboration tools, there is no guarantee that they will use them, or use them in the way you intended. Controlling Web interactions can be difficult; discussion boards and chat rooms are notorious for getting quickly off-topic. In addition, computer-based training has a history of being a platform for self-paced training. Your learners may carry that association (and the one from schooling that says "Do your own work") over to Web learning; it may not occur to them to interact. Like role-plays in a classroom, Web interactions may be seen by your learners as an exercise.

Solutions to the New Skill of Web Collaboration

Structure the interactions in Web learning so they are seen as real work. If you provide real problems for your learners to work on, they will see the Web as a way to build relationships and cross-functional knowledge that they can then access when dealing with real customers, real products, and real colleagues.

Provide a moderator (perhaps a senior manager) who can keep the Web discussions on track, and who can model collaborative behaviors by suggesting other employees the learners might bring into the collaboration (such as technical experts from other departments).

Pro #3: Better Use of Instructors

With Web publishing, the line between teacher and learner blurs in terms of who can contribute to the knowledge base. Access to experts is easier with the Web, as mentioned in the section on collaboration. Because the Web has so much information and its collaborative tools give employees direct access to the experts, some executives in your company may have arrived at the conclusion that you can get rid of all those expensive classroom instructors in your training department.

However, although the role of the instructor may change dramatically when you use the Web for learning, it does not go away. You may no longer need an instructor to deliver the content that you or the experts provide, but you will still need an instructor to help learners make sense of what the expert is saying. Experts usually do not make the best teachers, as anyone who has suffered through a brain dump from your company's technology or finance department, for example, can probably attest. Experts can deliver information, but often they cannot explain how to use it. You need instructors to translate between the expert and the learner.

The instructor has other roles to play in Web learning environments. Because of the high probability that your learners will suffer information overload, instructors must be available to help learners

- Ask the right questions (that is, frame useful Web searches).
- Evaluate the relevance, usefulness, and truth of the Web's information glut.
- Navigate the sea of Web links and not get lost.
- Create their own knowledge (rather than just learn someone else's) and publish it for others in the company to use.

Instructors in a Web learning environment also need to

- Structure and moderate learner discussions and chats.
- Show learners how to collaborate, even if they are never in the same physical place.

This last role of the instructor is crucial in a Web learning environment. Hiltz (1995, p. 8) found that "whether or not the [virtual classroom] mode is 'better' also depends crucially on the extent to which the instructor is able to build and sustain a cooperative, collaborative learning group; it takes new types of skills to teach in this new way."

Con #3: Instructors Unfamiliar with the Web

The problem with turning your classroom instructors into Web instructors is that, except for those who already teach with or about computer technology, they may not have the interest or ability to learn to use the Web. Many instructors enjoy the autonomy of building and delivering their own classes and of being the sole judge of a student's pass-or-fail success. Perhaps your company rewards instructors for being the purveyors of knowledge and the givers of grades, leaving them little time or incentive to learn to use the Web.

Solutions to Instructors Who Lack Web Experience

Start by pairing your classroom instructors with a technical specialist who can put their course materials on the Web for them. That way, the instructors can have the familiarity of seeing what their course looks like in a Web environment, without having to first learn the unfamiliar skill of how to put it there.

Have your instructors team-teach a Web course. It will model collaboration for their learners, and it will help the instructors not feel as though they are alone in trying to figure out how to teach without face-to-face contact.

Pro #4: Maximize Media Capability

Multimedia Web browsers remove the need for diverse and expensive peripheral devices, such as CD-ROM and laser disc players or video and audio cassette recorders. Using Web technology, you can do something that you could never do before as an educator: create, distribute, and display all the training media—video, sound, graphics, text, even a live instructor—in one environment, the Web browser. In a sense, the personal computer has become a player for the Web and all its media.

Con #4: Media Overload

Unfortunately, this leads to an irresistible temptation to use a plethora of media just because you can, without assessing their educational value. A similar problem occurred when desktop publishing first became widespread. Just because writers could use fifteen different fonts and put photographs and colored charts on the same page, they did so—and ended up creating some ugly and unusable documents.

The danger for Web learning is that, in many cases, showy multimedia presentations have become more important than well-designed instructional interactions. Conversely, because many word processing tools make it easy to convert documents to HTML, there is a temptation to just hang existing printed material on the Web without reconsidering how the content and format may need to change for a Web learning situation.

In short, the ease of creating complex multimedia on the Web may mean that you create ineffective training faster. And will your learners even see it?

Many Web media elements take so long to download that your learners may decide that the best way to use the Web is with the graphics turned off. Chapter Seven contains additional considerations for media presentations in Web learning environments.

Solutions to Media Overload

Make sure that your media elements (especially the large ones, such as video) are necessary for learning and are not just there to attract attention. Instead of assuming that your audience needs sound or full-motion video, try colored text or static pictures to maintain learners' interest.

If you do need several types of media in your Web learning environment, make sure that your learners have access to the technology to display them all efficiently.

Pro #5: The Web Seems Ubiquitous

The Web seems to be everywhere. Many of your company's employees are probably already savvy users of the Web. The same employees are also likely to have a variety of high-tech devices such as personal organizers and laptop computers that will provide them with access to a Web learning environment.

Con #5: Ubiquitous for Only a Few

But is the Web, with all of its attendant hardware, software, and wiring, actually part of your learners' work environment? Or will they still need to go to a specific place to learn, as they did with classroom training? The questions that you answered in Chapter Three about your learners' environment will prevent you from falling into the trap of believing that the Web is available anytime and anywhere for everyone in your learner group. While millions of users are connected to the Web, billions more are not. In addition, employees may not have their own computer or may not be in an environment that allows them to get to the Web when they most need to learn.

For example, can the mobile sales or service professionals in your company who are at customer sites or out in the field all day count on having a reliable Internet connection or even a reliable source of electricity? The just-in-time learning that the Web promises may not be possible in your workplace.

Solutions to the Unavailable Web

As part of your learner-technology assessment, determine when and where your employees learn now, and see if there is Web access (or even a computer) at that time and location.

Start your learning environment with employees who have Web access, know how to use it, and can learn a skill that they need by sitting in front of a computer. As your company develops experience with the value of Web-based learning, it will become easier to support the investment needed to make the Web available to employees who do not currently have sufficient access to make Web learning feasible.

Pro #6: Web Technologies Run on Many Types of Computers

By using many of the available tools for creating Web documents, you can create learning modules that will run on almost any computer that has a Web browser, without having to worry about what operating system or other applications are installed. Also, by using Web servers, you can create a lesson once, give it a Web address (a Uniform Resource Locator, or URL), and have instructors and learners access the original item from any place at any time. When it comes time to update materials, you only need to change one file, rather than re-mastering and sending out new manuals, disks, or CDs. Excess inventory of obsolete instructional materials is not an issue when you use the Web.

Con #6: Many Web Technologies Require Advanced Skills

The main problem with getting your learning materials to the Web is that the tools to do so often require more programming skill than most of their vendors will admit in their product literature. In addition, few of these tools have built-in instructional design; most focus on media production and not on creating learning environments through the use of instructional strategies.

Solution to Skill Shortages

An organization can build up skills incrementally—there's a great deal that can be done with a moderate knowledge base, without becoming an all-round expert. This book goes a long way toward addressing the instructional design aspects of the job. Tasks that require greater expertise than an organization has been able to build internally can be contracted out to freelance specialists, and here again, this book can help. It is much more efficient and economical to line up a job when you already know what needs to be accomplished than when you ask the outside expert to define the problem as well as the solution.

Pro #7: The Web Lowers Learning Costs

Studies are beginning to show that the cost savings of using the Web for learning can be real and immediate. The return on investment for corporate intranets (networks that use Internet technology within a company and that are set up so that only people within the sponsoring company can gain access to them) can be 1,000 percent in just six to twelve weeks, and if you use that intranet for your learning environment, it will cost you, on average, $46 per learner per year, compared to $66 per learner per year for traditional computer-based training (Paul, 1997).

Further, using the Web for learning

- Reduces travel time and cost for learners, experts, and instructors
- Probably will not require new hardware or software, especially for expensive peripheral multimedia devices
- Makes updating materials as easy as editing a Web page, rather than sending out hard copy revisions, disposing of the old material, and storing the new material

Con #7: The Web Raises Development Costs

The savings for Web learning mostly come during delivery; you can reach many more learners without incurring the classroom, travel, and equipment costs inherent in the traditional approach. However, these savings may be entirely offset by significant costs on the development end. Web learning, like other forms of computer-based training, still takes about two hundred hours for each hour of learning time, and requires expertise from several fields (Williams and Peters, 1997). In addition to instructional designers and instructors, creating your Web learning environment may require graphic artists, digital video and audio technicians, programmers, user interface designers, and a Webmaster to publish all the material and keep the server running.

This last aspect—the Web server—can make Web learning very expensive indeed. For mid- to large-sized corporations in 1997, the average cost to implement a Web server, including hardware, software, and content conversion, was $109,000 (Paul, 1997). After implementation, that same Web server costs $400,000 to $500,000 per year in upkeep, with half of that cost being spent on maintaining and updating the content (Miller, 1998, citing Jim Boyle, who has studied the topic of electronic document management extensively).

Solutions to the Expense of Web Learning Development

Keep your media elements to a minimum, at first. This will help you determine if you really need video and audio at all (as mentioned earlier). It will also keep your production costs down, as you will not need so many different media producers and their expensive equipment.

If your company already has server and networking hardware and software, it may be more cost-effective to buy time on the existing infrastructure rather than trying to install and maintain a separate Web learning network.

Making a Case for Web Learning

If you've worked through the steps recommended in Chapters Three through Five, you have learned how to conduct a learner-technology assessment to ensure that your audience and your work environment are ready for the Web

EXHIBIT 5.2. OUTLINE FOR
WEB LEARNING PROJECT PRESENTATION.

At some point, you will need to gain approval for—and get resources committed to—your Web learning project. You can use this template to pull together all of the information from Chapters One through Five into a presentation on why your company should use the Web to meet a learning need (or perhaps why it shouldn't do so).

1. A brief overview of how other companies/organizations use the Web for learning. (Use the information from Chapters One and Two to show that the Web is already being used for educational purposes.)

2. What employees of this company need to learn, and how the Web might help.
   • Results of needs assessment.
   • Results of learner-technology assessment. (List skills and content that could be learned via the Web, this company's current use of the Web, and why the Web would be accepted as a learning platform here—or why not.

3. The pros and cons of using the Web for learning in this company. (Use the answers to your questions from the "Web Learning Pros and Cons Worksheet" here.)

4. Recommendations about using (or not using) the Web for this learning project in our company.

EXHIBIT 5.3. THE PROS AND CONS OF USING THE WEB FOR LEARNING.

Web Characteristic	Pro	Con
Accessing Information	• Find information on almost any topic • Contact experts more easily • Get the latest information • Update and distribute information from one source • No inventory of (outdated) materials	• Difficult for learners to make sense of huge mass of information from links and searches • Easy to get lost following links
Collaboration	• Chat, discussions, and e-mail make time and space less of a barrier • Learners become part of a community • Enhances organizational learning and organizational memory	• Interactions are difficult to keep on track • Learners may not know how to behave (netiquette) or collaborate over a network
Role of Instructor	• Learners can become teachers by publishing their knowledge • Instructors can focus on helping learners collaborate with each other to make sense of information	• Instructors may have a strong attachment to their role as "the font of knowledge" • Instructors may not know how to use the Web for learning
Use of Media	• Only need one "player"—a Web browser—for most media	• Over-use of media • Most instructional development time spent on media production

EXHIBIT 5.3. *(continued)*

Web Characteristic	Pro	Con
		• Production value (glitz) more important than learning value
Ubiquitous Web	• Web seems to be everywhere • Most learners will have some familiarity with Web	• Web may not be part of everyday work • Access may not be possible when learning is most needed (in the field or internationally)
Need for Programming	• Web tools (such as HTML) allow Web documents to be created once and played on a variety of hardware and software platforms	• Tools require considerable programming skill • Commercial tools contain proprietary elements that may not play on all platforms
Cost of Web Learning	• Using the Web lowers the cost of maintenance, update, distribution, inventory, travel, and hardware	• Development takes a team of (expensive) specialists: graphic designers, programmers, media producers, Webmasters • Web servers are expensive to purchase and maintain

and why collaboration is important for adult learners, and you have seen some of the strengths and limitations of using the Web for learning. You can use the points presented in these chapters and the background in Chapters One and Two to make a business case to colleagues and executives about the best way to use the Web for learning in your company. Use the template in Exhibit 5.2 to outline your presentation.

FAST-GLANCE SUMMARY

Exhibit 5.3 summarizes the advantages and disadvantages of setting up a Web learning environment. The exhibit covers four key areas that will be important factors to the success of your Web learning environment:

- *Access:* Can your learners get to the Web?
- *Content:* Is the content learnable on the Web?
- *Technology:* Do you and your learners have the ability to use the Web?
- *Cost:* Can you really afford the Web?

To Learn More About . . .

Writing a business case for Web-based training:
Hall, B. (1997). *Web-based training cookbook.* New York: Wiley.

The changing role of instructors in technology-based education:
Young, J. R. (1997). Rethinking the role of the professor in an age of high-tech tools. *Chronicle of Higher Education,* http://chronicle.com/colloquy/97/unbundle/background.htm.

PART THREE

WEB LEARNING DESIGN STUDIO

Because the Web is awash with so much information, the most important decisions you will make about your Web learning environment pertain to how you organize and present the content for your learners. The information organization, or *architecture*, will influence almost every aspect of your Web site, including page design, navigation, and user interface. You want your users to learn something from the Web environment; that is, to be able to do their jobs differently and better because of the content you provide to them.

So, starting with the crucial area of content organization, the next four chapters present an integrated set of considerations that will guide you in creating your Web learning environment:

- Organizing content to enable learning (Chapter Six). You will need to structure and break up your content in ways that learners can master basic skills and concepts before moving on to more complex ones.
- Presenting content within the possibilities and constraints of the Web and the computer screen (Chapter Seven). Teaching is not the same as making a presentation. This chapter suggests ways to

ensure that your learners will pay attention to the material in the way you intended.

- Creating opportunities for learners to practice with the content (Chapter Eight). Learners need to be able to apply the skills they have learned, which may not always be possible on the Web.
- Assessing whether or not learning occurred, and to what extent the Web learning environment helped or hindered that learning (Chapter Nine). Your learners (and their managers) will want to know if they learned anything in the Web environment. Assessment is an area where the Web can make some unique contributions to learning, beyond simply putting the test on-line.

CHAPTER SIX

ORGANIZING CONTENT FOR WEB LEARNING

OBJECTIVES

After reading this chapter, you will be able to

- Explain why content organizing is particularly important for the Web learning environment.
- List types of content that are appropriate for Web learning.
- Describe at least two ways of organizing content for learning, and give examples of how that organization might appear on the Web.
- Use a Web template to apply content organization guidelines to the design of your own Web learning environment.
- Explain why Web technology makes content updating and maintenance easier.

Knowledge Versus Information

As Chapter Five noted, one of the problems with using the Web for learning is that very little of the Web's plethora of information is organized in a manner that creates knowledge. Unless you apply some organization to your content, the Web will not be an environment in which your employees can learn quickly and easily and in a way that allows them to perform better on the job. David Merrill, a leader in the instructional design and instructional technology fields, makes two observations that are especially relevant to the Web information glut and its effect on Web learning: "Information is not instruction" (1998, p. 37), and "You can't 'discover' your way to competence" (April 1997).

These two warnings are particularly applicable to Web learning, where so much content is available to your learners either through what you provide or through the browsing (discovering) that they will do on their own. Gordon (1997, p. 31) sums up the problem for learning that is caused by the plethora of information available on the Web: "What bothers skeptics is not the threat of page-turners so much as the idea of cobbling together training courses from a collection of found objects."

To prevent the "cobbling together" effect that Gordon mentions, you will need to select and stick to an instructional design strategy, paying particular attention to how you organize the learning content. Everything else in your Web learning environment depends on your instructional design and content architecture. Although the details of instructional design strategies are beyond the scope of this book (see the "To Learn More About" section at the end of this chapter for resources on the topic), content organizing schemes have such major implications for your Web learning site that they will be the focus of the remainder of this chapter.

Kinds of Content That Can Be Learned Using the Web

Almost any kind of content can be presented on the Web; the key consideration is whether or not learners can engage in meaningful practice with the content using the Web. (This concept will be discussed in detail in Chapter Eight.) The Web lends itself to learning in three broad areas of content: factual information, collaboration and group work, and human interaction skills.

Factual Information

The Web is a good vehicle for delivering factual content. This is especially true if that content is prerequisite to other types of learning activities. For example, learners can read the content on the Web before they arrive at a class. You can reduce the amount of time that learners spend in classrooms or labs by giving them the knowledge components on a Web site and devoting their in-class time to skills development and practice. This will also reduce the amount of time that your instructors need to lecture or deliver content and will give them more time to help learners individually. For instance, learners can read about the parts of a machine before they arrive at a hands-on class about how to fix it.

Collaboration and Group Work

The Web provides tools (such as discussions, chat rooms, and e-mail) for learning when collaboration and group work are important, especially among audiences who are dispersed in time or space. The Web's collaborative capabilities are particularly useful when group learning and problem solving are needed to solve unstructured or undeveloped issues (such as how to sell into global markets). For your learners, sharing their own experiences and perspectives on the problem may be even more valuable than learning the content you have prepared for the class. In addition, the Web can "let people who are unable or unwilling to meet face to face practice collaborating with each other over a computer network" (Management in cyberspace, 1998, p. 68).

Human Interaction Skills

The Web is emerging as a useful vehicle for learning and practicing human interaction skills. As you may have already experienced, a growing amount of interaction is taking place in cyberspace. Therefore, knowing how to behave on-line is an increasingly useful skill. In the past, when most human interaction was face to face, the best place to learn interpersonal skills was in a classroom; however, because many business interactions are now happening on-line, the Web is becoming a good place to learn how to interact when body language, tone of voice, and other interaction cues are missing.

Organization Strategies for Web Learning Content

Focusing first on content organization is not easy to do, especially when all the bells and whistles of Web technology beckon to you. However, becoming overwhelmed by the technology and dedicating too little time to the instructional and content organization aspects is one of major pitfalls of using the Web for learning (Driscoll, 1998).

Two aspects of Web technology are worth keeping in mind, because they will have opposite effects on your content organization:

1. *A key inhibitor in your Web learning environment is the size of the computer screen.* Breaking up the content into screen-size pieces that do not require much scrolling (especially on a laptop computer) becomes an important factor in content organization. To see a good example of compact, chunked content organization, take a look at any lesson at http://www.learn2.com, and answer the following questions:

- What is the average size of the text block? Note that you usually do not need to scroll to read the entire block.
- How is the text organized (phrasing, sentence structure, sentence order) in a way that is compact yet delivers useful instruction?
- How have graphics been organized to take up minimum space yet still be useful?

2. *The three-dimensional nature of the Web greatly expands your options.* Compared to a paper presentation, the Web makes it much easier to link the pieces of content together. Compared to either paper or CD-ROM, the Web makes it much easier to use content that other authors have already prepared—as long as it's been published on other Web sites, a simple link will make it available to your learners, too.

Assuming that you cannot fit the content that needs to be learned onto one Web page, what are your options for organizing the content in your Web learning environment? Jonassen, Grabinger, and Harris (1997) have catalogued 106 ways of organizing content to enable learning. Their list is a reminder that there are many creative ways to put content together so that your employees can learn new skills from it. Two well-documented content organization strategies that provide differing amounts of structure are described in the following sections, along with examples and implications for the Web learning environment.

Cognitive Model

The cognitive model of organization mixes content and learning activities early in the learning process. This model considers the outcome of one learning activity as valid content for the next one. In other words, each piece of content depends heavily on what the learner did in a previous exercise (Gillani and Relan, 1997).

The cognitive approach helps learners explore the content and bring their own structure to it. It requires active content management and flexible content restructuring, depending on what the learners are finding and creating. If you use a cognitive approach to your content, you will need a tracking mechanism within your Web site to monitor what each learner has seen and done so you can determine what they need to do next.

There are many cognitive models for organizing content for learning, but they all tend to have the same four major components.

Advance Organizer. This is more than an overview or introduction; it provides high-level contextual structure for what the employees are about to learn. An advance organizer will give them some mental hooks on which to hang specific pieces of content, as well as the rationale for learning it. Advance organizers give the why as well as the what of learning.

Example: Employees who are learning how to write marketing plans are provided with a context of the relationship between customer needs and company capabilities. This relationship is what drives the need for marketing plans.

Web implications: An advance organizer for content in a Web environment might include content from customers or from competitors' Web sites, followed by a visit to the product section of your company's intranet.

Model. This includes the major sections or organizing principles of the particular topic area. It can be an outline or a graphic that shows the pieces of something and how they fit together.

Example: Learners see an outline of your company's marketing plan template.

Web implications: The outline might be presented on one Web page. Each section of the outline might be a link to a definition of that section or to a list of key points that should be included in a marketing plan.

Exploration. Learners analyze examples, talk with the experts who produced them, and otherwise interact with the content to make their own sense of it.

Example: Learners are shown several examples of successful and unsuccessful marketing plans and are given opportunities to talk with marketing plan experts.

Web implications: Content on the Web site is organized into types of marketing plans. Each type links to a real plan that resulted in real products for your company. Plans are annotated so that learners can understand how they were developed. The authors of the plans are available by e-mail to answer learners' questions about how they created the plans.

Construction. Learners create their own work from the models that were presented. They may also change the models or create new ones and publish them so that they can be used in the course curriculum in the future.

Example: Learners write a marketing plan for a product that they believe the company needs to develop.

Web implications: Using asynchronous discussions and HTML editors, learners in various cities collaborate to create a marketing plan and publish it to a Web server. They edit the plan, as do senior marketing executives. The learners and the executives all contribute to a discussion about the merits and flaws in the plan. The final plan is posted to a restricted Web site, where selected customers are asked to provide feedback via e-mail on the product's potential in the marketplace. This content is included in the next Web-based class for new marketing employees.

Elaboration Model

The elaboration model gives specific guidance on how to divide, or elaborate upon, content. It is particularly useful for the considerable amount of chunking that you will need to do to fit content into the unique real estate of the Web. The elaboration model deals with three kinds of content: things, procedures, and processes (Reigeluth, Merrill, Wilson, and Spiller, 1994).

Content About Things.   Content that is about things can be organized into "kinds of things" that describe classifications or names (such as "laptops and mainframes are kinds of computers"), and "parts of things" that describe pieces or sections (such as "a keyboard and screen are parts of a computer"). Your learners usually need content about the names and parts of things before they can do something with them.

Example: Service technicians are learning how to fix computers. They need to be able to recognize what kind of computer they are fixing (such as laptop, server, mainframe), and which part is broken (such as hard drive, mouse, video board) so that they can apply the correct repair strategy or order the proper replacement part.

Web implications: Your learning Web site might have links to your company's on-line product catalog that has pictures and descriptions of different computers and their components. Rather than trying to keep up with changes in these products, you might simply use the catalog as your reference for current products and let the marketing department update your content for you.

Content About Procedures.   Content that is about procedures can be divided into "how to do" the procedure (such as step-by-step directions for fixing a computer) and "how to decide" which procedure to use (such as how to decide which part of the computer needs to be fixed). Procedures are the same things as skills, that is, they tell the learners what they are supposed to do.

Example: The step-by-step procedure for replacing the video board is described, as is the diagnostic procedure for deciding if the video board is defective.

Web implications: Take the information that is posted on your company intranet about customer complaints and organize your learning Web site around the major service problems. In addition, service technicians in the field contribute to an asynchronous discussion board about diagnostic and repair strategies that have worked successfully in the field. Your Web learning site links to the service department's discussion boards on the company's Web site.

Content About Processes.   Content that is about processes shows cause-effect relationships (such as "when you press this key, the computer sends a page to the printer"). Processes are what happen when learners apply their skills and do something to the content.

Example: The effect of plugging the video board into the correct and incorrect sockets is described and shown.

Web implications: Depending on whether they are connected to a fast or slow network, learners can choose between reading an HTML text file that describes the process in an if-then table or downloading a video clip that shows the results of placing the video board in various sockets.

Because you will have so much content to pare down and organize, the elaboration model also suggests three questions that will help you decide what content to put near the top or center of the computer screen on your learning site, and what to put in a "More About" or "Reference" section that you might link to the Web pages:

- What content pieces will learners need most often?
- What content pieces are critical to competent performance? In other words, if you left out a particular piece and learners then made a mistake because they did not have that knowledge, what would be the consequences of the error?
- How much does the content piece contribute to a larger understanding of the topic?

Jargon Alert: Knowledge Objects

Before we leave the topic of content organization, you should be aware that there is a growing effort to create software objects that contain content and strategies for learning. You may encounter such terms as *knowledge objects* or *learning objects.* The terms are borrowed from computer programming and refer to creating small pieces (objects) of code that fit together and work with one another, rather than creating huge applications with millions of lines of code that are difficult to revise, maintain, and fix. Knowledge objects are smaller pieces of content that a related "learning strategy object" would know what to do with; for example, a segment on how to repair computer video boards (the knowledge object) could be delivered as an HTML text page (a "lecture" learning strategy) or as part of a test question (an "assessment" learning strategy).

☙ ☙ ☙ ☙ ☙ ☙

Web Template: Content Organization

Exhibit 6.1 shows the first Web page of a tool that you can use to organize your Web learning content. This tool shows an example of the "Content About Things" organization strategy applied to learning the skill of computer repair.

You can use the template in Exhibit 6.1 to organize the opening page of content on your Web site. The advantage of using both text and graphics is that learners can either read or look at how the content is organized, and select whichever one fits best with their learning style.

Guidelines for Organizing Web Learning Content

To take advantage of the benefits that the Web offers to learning content, here are six guidelines for creating and organizing your content. As you begin to collect or create pieces of content for your Web learning environment, use these suggestions for each piece of content so that it will be most effective for your learners. Exhibit 6.2 includes these suggestions with more detail in a checklist format.

Focus on Action

Because you are creating learning for a workplace (that is, a place where learners need to apply the content), adopt a content organization strategy that focuses on doing rather than knowing. For example, instead of organizing the learning site by topic area, arrange it by skill area. The header on the home page might then be "How Do I . . . "—followed by a list of action links, such as "Write a marketing plan" or "Replace a video board." (A template for this type of presentation layout is in Chapter Eight.)

EXHIBIT 6.1. WEB CONTENT ORGANIZATION TEMPLATE.

This is the first page of a tool that you can use to organize your Web learning content. You can explore the links to see an illustration of the "Content About Things" organization strategy applied to learning the skill of computer repair.

- "Kinds of" computers are listed in the upper left block.
- "Parts of" computer hardware are listed next, both in a text list and then in a picture list (to accommodate at least two different learning styles).
- Depending on the choices that the learner makes in the "kinds of" and "parts of" lists, the main text and graphics field in the middle of the screen presents content on how to repair the device. The graphics and repair steps could include links out to the Web site of your company's service department.

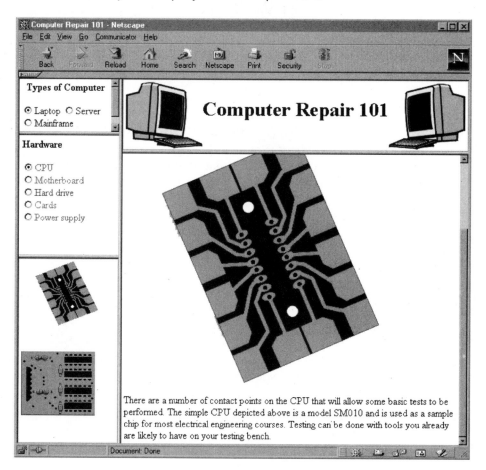

EXHIBIT 6.2. WEB CONTENT ORGANIZATION CHECKLIST.

As you collect and create the content for your learning Web site, make sure you have done the following tasks to organize the content:

Select the Organization Strategy

☐ If you want your learners to explore the content and discover or create meaning from it, the site uses the Cognitive Model.

☐ If your learners are new to the subject and need to know the names and pieces of things, the site uses the Content About Things model.

☐ If your learners need to know how to do a task, the site uses the Content About Procedures model.

☐ If your learners need to understand what happens when they do a task, the site uses the Content About Processes model.

Focus on Action

☐ The objectives state what learners will be able to do when they finish using the Web site.

☐ Each content piece states what the learner should do (read, write, discuss with a colleague, join the chat room).

☐ Web site navigation tells the learner what to do on each page, and where to go or what to do next.

Provide a Site Overview

☐ The site has a table of contents.

☐ The site has a guided tour or map that shows the learner all the major sections.

Use Consistent Vocabulary

☐ Terminology (such as labels, names, or titles) is consistent on every page.

☐ A glossary is linked to the site.

☐ Unfamiliar words are highlighted and linked to the glossary.

Allow Learners to Make Contributions

☐ Learners are given the path to the Web server and file where they can post documents.

☐ Learners are encouraged to participate in chats and discussions on-line.

(continued on next page)

EXHIBIT 6.2. *(continued)*

Explain the Content Architecture

☐ The table of contents or site map explains why the content was organized this way.

Use Hyperlinks Sparingly

☐ Links are attached to a few key words, rather to sentences or paragraphs.
☐ Backward links are provided so that learners can easily return to their starting point.

Provide a Site Overview

Because your learners will not be able to tell how large the learning environment is just by looking at the Web site (as they could with a binder or videotape), let them know what content is and is not included.

Use Consistent Vocabulary

Because you will not be able to lay all the pieces of the Web site side by side to check for consistency of content on all the pages, carefully choose a consistent vocabulary before you start creating Web pages. Make sure, for example, that you have not called the same document a "marketing plan" in one part of the site and a "marketing requirements document" in another.

Allow Learners to Make Contributions

Give learners an easy way to contribute to the content, either through discussions or by allowing them to publish to the learning Web site. This has two benefits. First, it takes some of the content creation burden off of your instructional designers. Because you cannot expect your instructional designers to be able to gather or keep current with all of the possible content, there needs to be a way for knowledgeable learners to contribute content that they know or have found. Second, contributing to the content is a way for learners to participate in the learning community (see Chapter Four).

Content contributions that you might ask learners to make include

- Here is some relevant information that I found at another Web site (ask learners to include the URL).
- Here is someone who is an expert who can help us (have learners provide the expert's e-mail address).
- Here is my own experience about what really works.
- Here is a new tool that I created.
- Here is my perspective on or understanding of the topic.
- Here is how I would reorganize the content in a way that works better for me.

Explain the Content Architecture

Explain the content organization model that you used. This will help the learner form a picture of what the content is about, as it shows learners at least one way to organize the whole content area. As Rosenfeld and Morville (1998, p. 34) found in their own efforts to create content architectures, "the power of a pure organization scheme derives from its ability to suggest a simple mental model for users to understand quickly."

Use Hyperlinks Sparingly

Keep external links to a minimum and make sure that they are relevant to the core content. It is very frustrating to learners to follow an interesting-looking link, only to discover that it is tangential to the content, and (worse) that they are now lost in cyberspace and can't get back to your site without going around to the home page.

Benefits of the Web for Content Creation and Maintenance

Working on the Web requires that you stay within the constrained area of the computer screen. Because of that, you will need to spend a considerable amount of time condensing and breaking up your content. However, the Web also offers several significant benefits to instructional content management.

Simplified Content Updating

Two major obstacles facing instructional designers are keeping the content updated and getting new content to learners. Web technologies have simplified both processes. Rather than having to interview the subject matter experts (SMEs) and then create all the learning content yourself, you can link to Web sites that SMEs have already created. The burden of content update lies with the SMEs, and your instructional designers can focus instead on updating the learning strategies and activities.

Also, by making content available on the Web, you can avoid distribution and inventory issues associated with hard copy materials. You no longer need to finish the content to meet a distribution deadline; you simply publish the content to the Web server as it is ready. Rather than sending content updates, you can just let learners know that new material is available, and give them the URL to the site.

Create Content Once for Many Computer Platforms

Web software languages such as Java and HTML run on a variety of computer platforms. Therefore, you only need to organize content once. Within certain limits, you no longer need to produce separate versions for the plethora of hardware and software configurations in your company. By using some advanced Web languages such as XML (eXtensible Mark-up Language) you can tag content for a variety of learning uses—from lectures to tests.

Sharing Best Practices

Organizational learning (or *organizational memory*) depends heavily on best practices. The Web makes creating and sharing best practices easier. Experts can publish their techniques, and learners can access them and then use the Web's collaborative tools to ask such questions as How did you do that? How did you get started? or What was the customer's reaction?

FAST-GLANCE SUMMARY

• How you organize the content that you need to teach has a significant impact on every other aspect of your Web learning environment, including presentation, learner activities, assessment, navigation, and user interface.

- Your content is constrained by the size of the computer screen, yet the Web gives you a three-dimensional capability that allows you to easily link to other content sources.
- Two common ways to organize content include
  The less structured "cognitive" approach, in which the learner explores and discovers the content
  The more structured "elaboration" approach, which organizes content into types, parts, steps, decisions, or cause-effect relationships
- Sustainable maintenance of content is always a problem in instructional design. The Web offers a significant advantage in allowing you to update the content in one place, without the concern of distribution and inventory of new content.

To Learn More About . . .

Information architecture:

Rosenfeld, L., & Morville, P. (1998). *Information architecture for the World Wide Web*. Sebastopol, CA: O'Reilly.

Knowledge architecture:

ID2 Research (Utah State University, School of Education, Department of Instructional Technology)—http://www.coe.usu.edu/it/id2.

Elaboration theory:

Merrill, M. D., & Twitchell, D. G. (Eds.). (1994). *Instructional design theory*. Englewood Cliffs, NJ: Educational Technology Publications.

Content and document management:

Bielawski, L., & Boyle, J. (1996). *Electronic document management systems*. Princeton, NJ: Prentice Hall.

Association of Information and Image Management International (AIIM)—http://www.aiim.org.

CHAPTER SEVEN

PRESENTATION STRATEGIES FOR WEB LEARNING

OBJECTIVES

After reading this chapter you will be able to

- Describe two different Web learning presentation strategies.
- Apply instructional presentation strategies to your Web content.
- Describe how Web technologies have both positive and negative impact on Web learning presentations.

Learning-Centered Presentation Strategies for the Web

Now that you have organized the content that your learners need, the next steps are to decide how you want to present the content to learners and what you want learners to do with it. This chapter describes instructional presentation strategies and their implications for a Web learning environment. Chapter Eight describes learning and practice activities.

The three-dimensional nature of the Web can help you get away from the linear metaphors of book pages and recording tape that characterize other instructional presentation strategies. On the Web, many presentation sequences are available besides "Previous" and "Next." And the next presentation does not need to reside on your Web site. Esque (1998, p. 46) describes a presentation sequence for teaching service technicians how to repair equipment: "After a procedural decision tree is exhausted, a button press might take the user to any number of Web locations that always contain the very latest developments regarding a specific product technology, market or whatever."

You have a choice of several instructional presentation strategies. Merrill (1994) suggests four major instructional presentation strategies—Tell, Show, Let, and Ask—that generally correspond to the traditional instructional presentation strategies of lecture, demonstration, practice, and assessment. However, these presentation strategies can be greatly enhanced in a Web environment.

The four strategies are listed in subsequent sections, with examples and implications for a Web learning environment.

The Tell Strategy

This strategy is appropriate for the factual content in your Web learning environment. The factual content is often the prerequisite to skills learning. The advantage of the Web is that a Tell instructional strategy does not mean just a text lecture on-line.

The Tell presentation strategy is good for teaching about the names and parts of things, and therefore is appropriate if you are using the organization strategy for Content About Things (see Chapter Six). For example, "telling" service technicians about the parts of a computer could include

- A text list of the parts
- Annotated pictures of the parts
- An audio clip describing the parts

Clicking on the pictures could bring up the text descriptions, and vice versa. Both the text and the pictures could offer the option of listening to a description.

There are some distinct advantages to using the Web for the Tell presentation strategy. Because the Web is a multimedia player, learners can have several presentation options available from one computer. This is helpful if you have an audience with diverse learning styles. Learners will have the option to read, listen, or look at graphical representations. In addition, the

Web can reduce the amount of time that your instructional designers spend creating and maintaining Tell presentations. Because these types of presentations have often been created by another department (such as product development or marketing), your designers may be able to simply add a learning structure (such as an advance organizer) to that material, and spend more of their time on the other presentation strategies that contribute to skill development.

The Show Strategy

This strategy is effective for the how-to-do-it procedure content and the cause-effect process. This strategy can also be used with content that shows learners how to decide which procedure to use, especially when visual or auditory cues are necessary to making the decision.

Again, because of Web technology, Show need not be confined to a videotape demonstration. A Show presentation strategy might include an expert service technician illustrating a detail of a repair strategy on a shared whiteboard in a synchronous Web classroom, or a simulation of what various computer problems look and sound like, so that the technician can learn which symptoms might indicate that the computer's hard drive needs to be replaced. This could be done using a Java applet.

Because computers have long been used for presenting simulations to learners, the "Lessons From the Field" section of this chapter contains an interview with an expert in Web-based learning simulations. The interview will give you some practical ideas and suggestions about using simulations in your own Web learning environment.

LESSONS FROM THE FIELD

Using Simulations in Web Learning Presentations

Larry Tesler is president of Stagecast (http://www.stagecast.com), a company that helps educators build visual interactive simulations for the Web and other platforms. The company provides tools to create simulations, models, games, stories, and lessons on the Web. Learners can then change and add to the simulations, based on their own knowledge and experience. Before coming to Stagecast, Tesler was vice president and chief scientist at Apple Computer, where he worked with Apple Classrooms of Tomorrow. He also spent several years with the Learning Research Group at Xerox's Palo Alto Research Center.

KEY POINTS

Tesler's Key Points About Web Learning Simulations:

- Separating simulations into one common player that will run various smaller models is a practical way to get around the bandwidth issues typically associated with computer-based simulations.
- Java is a useful programming language for creating Web learning simulations, as the output will run on a variety of hardware and software platforms.
- Learners need to be able to change the simulation itself in order to clearly understand cause and effect.

Advice for Using Simulations in Web Learning Environments

Tesler: Some day, the Internet will be accessible at high speed from anywhere on the planet. Until then, one strategy a training organization can adopt is to deploy simulation platforms that will function whether or not the learner is connected to the Internet. Java is an appropriate vehicle because it can run on a variety of hardware and software platforms, and will run whether or not the learner happens to be connected to the Internet at the time.

One way to keep limited bandwidth from constraining performance is to divide simulation software into two parts: a standard player common to all simulations and a file that contains the specifics of a particular simulation. (For example, the player could have the rules for all of the characters in a simulation, and the file could contain the characters that are specific to that simulation.) The standard player, which can be several megabytes in size, is installed once on each client computer as a Java class library. By sharing common code, most simulations will measure in kilobytes and download quickly through the Net.

How Learners Can Use Web-Based Simulations

Tesler: In a learning environment, what sets the computer apart from older media is its ability to simulate any system, simple or complex, scientific, social, or mechanical. Interactivity allows the student to pose what-if questions to a simulation and instantly and safely discover outcomes through graphic visualization.

A learner can explore a simulation at several levels. For example, a student should be able to change simulation parameters and add or remove components. Such what-if experiments help to develop an intuitive sense of cause and effect. The student should also be able to "open the hood" of the model, view the rules that make it tick, change rules, and define entirely new components. Altering a simulation depends on a student's understanding of the modeled system. Higher-order thinking skills come into play.

If a simulation is trivial or unapproachable, students will not use it. A practical technique is to introduce a system through a series of models that gradually increase in complexity. A learner can master one aspect of the system at a time. A staged approach also reminds the student of the difference between a model and reality.

What It Takes to Create Web-Based Simulations for Learning

Tesler: To create a Web-based learning simulation, you should select a sofware tool that allows "authoring by demonstration." This means that the simulation author describes the model in the same visual terms that the learner will experience.

The tool also should allow you to later alter the simulation's rules to make them more or less general, to add or relax conditions, to introduce randomness, or to generate quantitative reports. It is easier when all of this can be done using direct manipulation on concretely represented components. The tool should also allow the finished simulation to be published directly to the Web, without needing any conversion.

Advice for Creating Web Learning Environments

Tesler: Remember that discussion groups are as important a feature of the Internet as e-mail and the Web. Trainees can discuss problems and solutions as a team. A trainer can tap into on-line discussions to provide advice and assess student progress.

Also, it is true that judiciously chosen graphics and short audiovisual clips can enhance the impact of hyperlinked Web pages; however, the Web today is as different from television as it is from paper. Each medium should be used for what it does best. The Web offers the world of training several advantages over older media, including personalization, automated assessment, links to internal and external resources, and the computer's power to simulate.

The Let Strategy

This is the practice strategy, and you need to be careful when using it in your Web learning environment. As mentioned earlier, the Web probably will not be your complete practice environment because, for most of your learners, it is not their work environment. In that case, you can tell them and show them the content on the Web, but you can't arrange for them to use it in a realistic manner. However, if your audience consists of programmers, system engineers or Webmasters, the Web is the perfect presentation, practice, and assessment environment for them, as the Web is where they do their work.

Barlow (1998, p. 47) has suggested that a significant piece of the practice environment is the ability to ask about the content. "The difference between information and experience is this: You know you're having an experience if you can ask questions." The Web's collaborative tools, in particular, have a contribution to make to this instructional presentation strategy. Suppose, for example, that your learners practice skills—say, equipment repair—in a non-Web environment such as a computer lab. The Web can still help to make that experience more real for them in at least two ways.

- *Experts in field locations can use asynchronous discussion or e-mail to respond to learners' questions.* In the equipment repair example, field technicians could respond to questions about how equipment breaks and which procedure works to fix it in the real world. Learners can then go back and try these strategies in the lab. Your presentation strategy might simply be to provide a template for learners and experts to use for their e-mail messages.

- *Learners can use Web-published documents from other departments to answer questions about the context of what they are doing.* For example, the repair technicians might access the marketing department's home page to answer the question, How did we expect customers to use this piece of equipment?

The Ask Strategy

This is the assessment piece, and as with the Let strategy, the Web probably will not be the place where you ask learners to demonstrate their competence. Knowledge tests such as true-false or multiple-choice can be given on-line, but the Web has no advantage over other computer-based testing systems for these kinds of assessments.

What the Web can contribute to the Ask strategy is easy access to a community of evaluators. For example, if the skill to be learned is how to write a marketing plan, the "test" for your learners might require them to work as a group to write a marketing plan for a new product. The Web is an appropriate forum for collaboration on creating the plan, especially if the learners are in different locations. How they collaborate with each other and work with Web-published documents on this test is the same as how they will collaborate and share on real work projects. The Web is also an appropriate forum for convening a panel of marketing executives who might, for example, annotate the Web-published plan. (Chapters Eight and Nine include templates for this type of activity.) The executives might also use a moderated asynchronous discussion to give feedback to the learners.

Using the Web Template to Create Your Presentation Strategy

Using Web technology, you can put the presentation strategies together so that learners can choose different ways to learn the same content. For example, you can tell a programmer about HTML, you can show HTML code and its effects on text and graphics, and you can let learners ask expert programmers about HTML through asynchronous discussions.

Use the Web template in Exhibit 7.1 to create a template for your presentation strategy. Take the content that you organized in Chapter Six and select the best presentation strategy to go with it. For example, the Tell and Ask presentation strategies are good for factual content (tell the learners a fact and then ask them about it). The Show and Let strategies are good for procedure content (show learners a step and then let them try it). The Show strategy is good for process content (show learners what happens as a result of the procedure they just did).

Common Pitfalls in Web Learning Presentations

The strategies presented thus far will help you make sure that your audience can learn what they need from your Web presentations. There are also five presentation strategies that, although tempting to use, will make learning difficult for your audience:

- *Do not convert word processing documents to HTML and put them on a Web site.* If you are being pressured to put all of your company's training on the Web, this is the quickest way to do it. You can take the word processing documents that you created for your company's classroom courses, save them in HTML, and publish them on your Web site. The downside to this strategy is that much of the learning value is lost. The learner does not get to do much more than click and scroll, and all the interaction disappears. There was a reason you chose classroom instruction in the first place; moving that existing course to the Web requires you to rethink the presentation strategy if you want the same learning to occur.
- *Do not start by designing Web pages and navigation.* It is very tempting to start by designing the buttons and icons for your Web site presentation—these are the elements that have the most visual appeal. The problem with starting your design with these elements is that they focus your attention on the end-points (the pages), rather than on the structure and organization of how the content fits together. The learning flow, not the page flow, should be what determines your presentation. You need to figure out what content and tasks are needed, and in what order. Then decide if buttons or arrows or links will be needed.

EXHIBIT 7.1. WEB PRESENTATION STRATEGY TEMPLATE.

This is the first page of a tool that you can use to implement your Web learning strategy. These are the key features of the site:

- In the upper left corner, learners can choose to learn about HTML or XML.
- Using the four buttons across the top, learners can then choose

What or Why: These are Tell presentation strategies that describe what HTML/XML is and why you would want to write programs using it.

How: A Show presentation strategy that demonstrates how to write HTML code, and what the results look like. (This section could also include an Ask strategy that tests programmers' ability to write a piece of HTML code to produce a specified result.)

Where: A Let presentation strategy that refers learners both to code that they can try for themselves (such as the "3.2 version") and to experts ("Dave Raggett") who can help them.

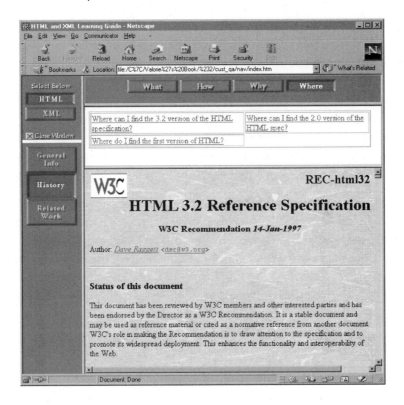

- *Do not use lots of graphics.* Graphics get attention, but are they really necessary for learning? And beyond the learning question, you need to consider if learners will have the technology to support the graphics. What runs seamlessly on your high-end computer may not work on a learner's laptop over a remote network. As Rossett and her team discovered, "Big, colorful graphics look wonderful to the creators, but take far too long to load and view. By the time the page is up, the user is gone" (Rossett, Keenan, and Adgate, 1997, p. 24).

- *Do not put the whole learning environment on the Web.* Historically, instructional design has tended to use one medium; all presentations had to be put in one environment such as classroom or CD-ROM because it was too expensive and time-consuming to design multiple environments. Although the Web can play all the traditional educational media, by itself it cannot be a complete learning environment simply because it is not the work environment for the majority of your employees. Your presentation strategy, therefore, should point learners to non-Web instructional resources, rather than trying to cram everything into HTML and onto the computer screen. Web learning environments do not need to be self-contained.

- *Do not confuse* presentation *and* instruction. As you plan how you will present the content on your learning Web site, you need to keep in mind that you are creating knowledge, not just delivering information. In other words, you want your learners to do something with the information, not just receive it. This distinction between presentation and instruction is crucial for your learning environment because how you measure the success of presentations is quite different from how you measure instruction.

A presentation is completed when the presenter is finished talking. In traditional presentations, success is often measured by the presenters' "stage presence" and how well they used various media elements. However, this is not how "instructional" presentations are measured. Instruction is measured in terms of reception, not just delivery. The crucial question for instruction is not, How well did you deliver the content? but How well did they learn the content?

In short, you need to keep the focus on instruction in your Web learning environment. Your instructional presentation strategies will prevent you from repeating the problem with much computer-based training: hours of isolation for the learner in front of a computer screen, with not much more activity than clicking "Back" and "Next."

To make sure that you are considering the learning elements at least as much as the media elements, ask yourself the reality check questions as you plan the presentations in your learning Web site.

Reality Check for Web Learning Presentations

- Do you learn from presentations like this?
- Do you know anyone who does?
- Are you sure that you could learn what you are expecting others to learn from this presentation?

𝓢𝓸 𝓢𝓸 𝓢𝓸 𝓢𝓸 𝓢𝓸 𝓢𝓸

Hints for Media and Navigation in Web Learning Presentations

This book is not about creating media or designing user interfaces for the Web; however, there are three considerations in these areas that will have a direct effect on learning, and will therefore affect your instructional presentations:

Bandwidth

Remember that video and audio, and even large HTML text files, may take a long time to download, especially over slower networks. Media variety can be motivating to learners, and may keep them engaged—but not if they have turned sound and graphics off so as to speed up the performance of their Web browser. Make sure that learners can still have the experience that you planned with your instructional presentation strategies, even if they cannot get all of the media elements. This is especially important for the Show strategies.

Use of Sound

Despite the warning about bandwidth and the common belief that sound in computer-based learning is a frill, some recent research indicates that sound is an important component in instructional presentations. Horton (1997, p. 19) reports that research subjects who viewed identical computer displays "consistently said that the one with better sound had a better picture."

Navigation

If your instructional presentation prescribes or suggests a path through the Web site, remember that how learners navigate influences what they learn. There is nothing so disruptive to learners as getting lost in cyberspace, and it is easy to become lost on the Web. Your presentation strategy must include information that shows your learners where they are in the content, where they need to go next, how to get back to previous content for review and how to leave without losing their place. The combination of content organization and instructional presentation determines the navigation strategy for your learning Web site.

꙰ ꙰ ꙰ ꙰ ꙰ ꙰

FAST-GLANCE SUMMARY

- The measure of success of your Web learning presentation is not how well the multimedia elements were presented but how well your audience learned.
- Your presentation strategy always needs to provide context for the learners, as it is so easy to get lost on the Web. One way to help your learners is to explicitly show them the model (as a site map, for example) that you used to organize the content. This will also help them make their own model of the content.
- Four instructional strategies for presenting content include
  —Tell (giving learners information)
  —Show (presenting a demonstration)
  —Let (giving learners a structured way to work with the content)
  —Ask (assessing learners' skill and knowledge of the content)

- Five temptations to avoid in Web learning presentations include
  —Converting text documents from other types of training (such as from classroom binders) to HTML and putting them on a Web site
  —Starting your presentation design by designing pages and navigation elements
  —Using too many graphics
  —Trying to get the entire learning environment on the Web
  —Making a presentation instead of giving instruction

To Learn More About . . .

Learner motivational factors:

Cornell, R., & Martin, B. L. (1997). The role of motivation in Web-based instruction.
In B. Khan (Ed.), *Web-based instruction* (pp. 93–100). Englewood Cliffs, NJ: Educational Technology Publications.
Duchastel, P. (1997). A motivational framework for Web-based instruction. In B. Khan (Ed.), *Web-based instruction* (pp. 179–184). Englewood Cliffs, NJ: Educational Technology Publications.

CHAPTER EIGHT

WEB LEARNING ACTIVITIES

OBJECTIVES

After reading this chapter you will be able to

- Differentiate practice activities that can and cannot be conducted on the Web.
- Determine whether your learners need to know the information itself, or know where to find it.
- Select individual and collaborative learning activities that are appropriate for a Web learning environment.

The Problems of Practice on the Web

The two preceding chapters showed how your choice of content organization and instructional presentation strategies greatly influences how you design your learning Web site. Those two chapters focused on what the instructional design needs to do to help learning happen. This chapter focuses on an equally critical element, giving the learners the opportunity to practice the skills that the content has taught them. To turn information into knowledge and skill, your learners must have the opportunity for real practice with the content.

One problem is that the Web cannot provide many real-world practice activities. There has been a rush to get training to the Web without considering how to provide practice. Sherry and Wilson (1997, p. 70) reported, "in [Web-based] instructional activities, we have found erratic differences in learning outcomes among participants." These differences are due to the lack of opportunities that most Web learning environments are able to give for actually using the skills that are taught there.

A second problem in putting learning practice activities on the Web is that Web-based learning simulations are often difficult to author and take a considerable amount of bandwidth to download and play. The technology and speed of the Web just are not good enough yet to warrant the considerable programming skill and expense required to create simulations that replicate hands-on practice. (See Larry Tesler's interview in Chapter Seven for some comments on a brighter future for Web-based learning simulations.) In short, the Web probably cannot provide the practice environment that your learners will need to demonstrate competence in many of their workplace skills.

The Opportunity for Web-Based Activities

However, because of its collaborative capabilities and three-dimensional nature, the Web can facilitate learning activities that are difficult or impossible in other environments. The Web can be used for exploratory and collaborative learning, and for asking questions and getting almost immediate answers from distant locations and experts—activities that are more valuable than the library searches or small-group interactions that have been used in traditional training. There are huge learning advantages to being able to access the world's digital library, and to communicate in real time or asynchronously with experts and fellow learners all over the planet.

Why Using a Computer Is Not a Learning Activity

However, much traditional computer-based learning has not had the Web's capabilities, nor has it been designed for more than one learner in front of a computer. Much of the activity in traditional CBT has centered around using the computer. Some CBT claims that this is "interaction," in the sense that the learner does something and gets a response. However, it is not *trans-action,* which is all about sharing something of value (such as knowledge) and creating meaning from it. With its collaborative tools, the Web has a tremendous capacity to facilitate transaction learning activities, but you may need to overcome your learners' (low) expectations that most of their interaction with the learning experience will be about manipulating the mouse and keyboard to trigger the next media element.

Real learning activities address the question of how information becomes knowledge and skill. And the answer for your Web learning environment should not be "By pointing and clicking and browsing." Learning a workplace skill means that employees need the opportunity to practice with the content to produce something, such as a marketing plan, computer code, or repaired machine. Pointing and clicking are navigational activities, not learning practice activities (unless the task in question is learning how to point and click). Further, undirected Web browsing can be distracting and frustrating, especially for novice learners.

What you do not want, and what this chapter will help you avoid in your own Web learning environment, is a new twist on an old adage about learning activities:

I hear and I forget.
I see and I remember.
I do and I understand.
I point and click and I point and click.

Deciding Where the Knowledge Needs to Reside

There is a crucial—and often overlooked—factor that will help you decide which learning activities you need to provide and whether or not the Web can help. Spend some time thinking about the following question, which is key to determining how much and what kind of practice your learners will need:

- For this particular content and skill area, which is more important for employees: knowing the information, or knowing where to find it?

This is Norman's (1988) distinction between "knowledge in the head" and "knowledge in the world," and it has significant implications for the Web learning activities that you design.

- Knowledge in the head (memory) is more efficient, but you have to learn it first, and then practice using it.
- Knowledge in the world requires less work (you do not have to remember it), but you have to find it first—and efficient "finding" also requires practice.

Knowledge Needs to Be in the Heads of Your Learners If . . .

- Looking up the information will cause an unacceptable delay (a paramedic should not be looking up basic life-saving information).
- Reference materials cannot easily be taken to or accessed from the work area (an electrical line repair person cannot take manuals or computers to the field in wet weather).
- Using references will cause credibility problems (a salesperson cannot look up basic product information in front of a customer).

Knowledge Can Stay in the World If . . .

- Memorization is not necessary (the paramedic does not need to remember hospital phone numbers).
- Its location is obvious or well-known (the electrical line repair procedure is printed on the electrical box).
- The information changes frequently (the salesperson is better off not trying to remember prices, as giving out-of-date information to a customer could cause PR problems or even obligate the company to deliver at a price below current levels).

৯৯ ৯৯ ৯৯ ৯৯ ৯৯ ৯৯

Often, instructional designers wish to equip learners for every possibility, to train them on every bit of information and every permutation of a skill. Yet there is never enough time to create, deliver, and learn the lengthy courses that would result from such a wish. Especially in a Web-enabled world, there is just too much information that changes too rapidly. Learners will have an increasingly difficult time storing and using all the relevant data that is available.

Unfortunately, learning activities usually do not include where to find information. Worse, traditional testing requires that knowledge be in the head—using a resource is regarded as cheating. Yet "industry studies show that office workers will generally spend 100–200 hours a year looking for information" (Miller, 1998, p. 33, quoting Jim Boyle). It seems, then, that a fruitful activity would be for learners to practice how to effectively and efficiently find information—an activity where the Web can make a great contribution. Although casual browsing is rarely a productive learning or workplace activity, conducting good searches is useful. An appropriate learning activity would be to have your learners develop and practice effective Web search strategies.

Another benefit of using the Web for learning activities is that it facilitates taking knowledge "in the head" and putting it "in the world." Through Web-page publishing and collaborative tools, experts can put the knowledge that is in their heads into the world. Learners can find it, bookmark it, and leave it where they can get back to it easily without having to remember either the information itself or exactly where to find it on the Web.

Exhibit 8.1 shows the opening screen of a Web template that you can use for organizing both "knowledge in the head" (learning) and "knowledge in the world" (finding) activities. This type of site is called a *portal* page, a Web term that means that the page's main purpose is to link to other sites. A portal page is a good way to organize learning activities because it presents learners with all of their activity options in one place. Learners can choose what they want to do, rather than spending time looking for content. For example, the learner addressed in the template could choose to take courses that teach skills (such as programming or managing) that she will eventually need to have on tap all the time, and to read articles containing useful background information without bothering to memorize it.

- *Knowledge in the head:* A list of courses recommended for this learner. The courses are listed in the left frame, and a calendar of those courses is conveniently displayed at the bottom.
- *Knowledge in the world:* A list of articles relevant to the learner's current needs. These articles are listed in the upper right frame. The links will stay available so the learner can read the articles and leave them where they are, to be reread if she ever needs details beyond those that happen to stick.

A Model for Web Learning Activities

Learning activities apply primarily to the Let presentation strategy, as that is the strategy in which learners try out and experiment with new skills. So, what kinds of practice activities can you design for the Web? Snyder (1997) suggests the four-part model illustrated in Exhibit 8.2. (The example of "learning how to write a marketing plan" continues from preceding chapters.)

Learning Activities on the Web

Snyder's model gives four areas of learning activities (discovery, invention, production, and generalizing) that apply to the Web and other learning environments. You might use the model to plan the entire set of activities for your learners, so that you will not feel trapped into trying to get all of the practice onto a computer screen. It is all right to send your learners to experiential activities that are not on the Web!

Specific activities that might fit into any one of the four areas can be divided into *collaborative* and *individual* activities, with the former being perhaps the most important to workplace learning. As Snyder (1997, p. 8) found, "the most effective way to manage . . . competence is not to codify

EXHIBIT 8.1. "LEARNING" AND "FINDING" ACTIVITIES TEMPLATE.

This is the opening screen of a Web template that you can use for organizing both "knowledge in the head" (learning) and "knowledge in the world" (finding) activities.

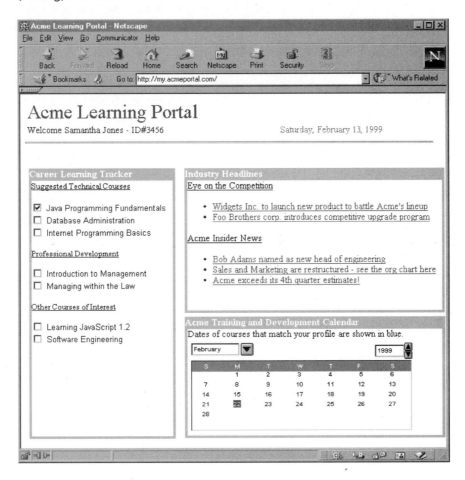

EXHIBIT 8.2. A MODEL FOR WEB LEARNING ACTIVITIES.

Type of Learning Activity	Definition	Web Learning Activity Examples
Discovery	Learners identify the general scope and content of a company's problems and opportunities.	• Search the Web for information on the market that your company is in, and describe the problems and opportunities that the industry as a whole is facing. • Join the Customer Service department's Web chat room and analyze customer issues and complaints about current products.
Invention	Learners develop ideas and approaches to solve problems.	• Access a competitor's Web site and evaluate how, or if, its products have solved a particular problem that your company or the industry is facing. • Moderate an asynchronous discussion about the problem with some of your company's strategic thinkers.
Production	Learners apply ideas and approaches to meet workplace requirements.	• Create a marketing plan for a product that will address the problem you identified. Publish it on the company intranet. • Ask senior marketing managers to comment on the plan by using an HTML editor so that readers can see who made which comments.
Generalizing	Learners document, interpret, and	• Document the strategy that you used to investigate the problem

disseminate their competence using, groupware, training, apprenticeships, and other transfer methods.	and publish it on the company's intranet.
	• Create an asynchronous Web "class" or new employees in the marketing department so that they can learn your methodoloqy and discuss it with you.

Source: Types and definitions from Snyder, 1997, p. 10.

it, but rather to engage members in continuous, informal learning processes that provide competence components as required, through story-telling, dialogue, peer coaching and shared practice."

It is with these collaborative activities that the Web can make a unique contribution to learning in your company. The "Lessons from the Field" section of this chapter illustrates the importance of collaborative learning activities in an interview with Dean Hovey, who is doing pioneering work in the teaching of collaborative business skills on the Web.

LESSONS FROM THE FIELD

Using Structured Discussion Groups in Web Learning Environments

Dean Hovey is director and senior vice president of marketing at Pensare (http://www.pensare.com), a company that creates intranet-based perform-ance courses on management, sales, marketing, finance, and customer serv-ice. The company uses a design model that emphasizes business content, knowledge sharing, and performance support tools. Pensare's Web learning environments employ structured discussions (also known as MUDs—multi-user discussions or dialogues) in which communities of learners within a com-pany come together to learn and share best practices. Dean has spent many years with venture capital firms and has founded several high-technology companies.

⌨ K E Y   P O I N T S

Hovey's Key Points About Using Structured Discussions for Web Learning:

- Structured discussions (also known as MUDs) are a type of simulation that provide enhancements and structure to an already-popular use of the Web: chat rooms (on-line areas where users can talk with each other by typing out their messages in real time).
- Structured discussions are appropriate for learning soft skills. Although the face-to-face aspects are absent, the rest of the interaction can be just as rich. In addition, many soft skills are now applied on the Web (in chat and e-mail), which makes the Web ideal for learning interaction skills for that environment.
- We need to learn how to design interactions, rather than using the Web as we have used other technologies.

How Structured Discussions Can Be Used in Web Learning Environments

Hovey: The term MUD originated with programmers who came together to create simulated virtual worlds on the Internet. These worlds were mostly described textually. Any number of people could enter the world simultaneously to role-play. The MUD world is constructed with a database and rules that the computer applies to the data to give form to the virtual world and to structure participants' interactions. One of the best-known early MUDs was set up so people could play the game Dungeons and Dragons on-line.

As it turns out, one of the Web's biggest successes is chat. MUDs add structure, context, and rules for interaction to the chat situation. Using the Web, this structure can be described by graphics and audio as well as text. Participants can play out scenarios and practice a real-world situation without the penalty of making real mistakes. They can practice with other people or with simulated personalities in the MUD.

Web-based MUDs can provide the richness of interaction without the associated travel time and cost. In addition, MUDs can take place even if some of the players are not available to participate. Role-play robots can be created to substitute for absent players.

Suggestions For Designing Educational Web-Based MUDs

Hovey:
- *Be clear about the intended outcomes.* For example, in a MUD with simulated executives, the outcome might be to help salespeople get appointments with top corporate decision-makers. The intent is to allow participants to run through several possible scenarios so that they feel comfortable with what might occur, rehearse techniques, experience their effect, and build confidence and instinctive reactions so that their first real calls will be successful.
- *Keep it short and simple.* Most of us do not feel we have time to play games, nor are we willing to commit to an exercise that we know will take a lot of time.
- *Keep it fresh and changing.* It is much better to let the learners choose to do the short MUD simulation as many times as they need than to make them commit to a long one. But if the short one is always the same, people quickly learn the outcome and become bored.
- *Give feedback often.* Give coaching tips often as learners make their decisions. It is frustrating to invest time in a conversation and not know how you are doing.
- *Provide choices.* To keep participants oriented and moving forward toward specific learning goals, give them more choice (but few completely open-ended decisions).
- *Mix the obvious with the subtle.* Subtle changes in the simulation (such as in how one character behaves) cause participants to think more deeply, which matures their understanding. The obvious helps participants experience success.

Why the Web Is an Appropriate Environment for Learning Soft Skills

Hovey: There is a belief that soft skills can only be learned through action experiences, such as role-play, where learners step into an active, participative role. It is a proven fact that if you get people to apply what they are learning immediately, to actually use it or do it, then learning and retention dramatically increase. This immediately raises the question of how to simulate the soft skill development experiences except through the use of live, face-to-face role-playing.

We know that there are other forms of media communication, such as TV, radio, and novels, that convey stories and situations that cause emotion and engagement. With all of these media—video, audio, graphics, and the written word—effectively combined within the delivery capability of Internet technologies, plus the interactive capability and potential for simultaneous collaboration, why would soft skills training not be an excellent candidate for the Web? Although the Web does not offer real face-to-face meetings, one of the wildfire successes of the on-line world is the tremendous amount of use of chat and dynamic interactions, of which MUDs are simply an enhancement. Chats are filled with all types of interaction, emotion, role-playing, and the exchange of information, ideas, and knowledge. This is proof enough that this technology can engage learners effectively in a way that works for soft skills training.

Major Barriers to Implementing Web Learning in the Workplace

Hovey: It is important to acknowledge that there is a tremendous interest in Web learning. Most training organizations know that it is impossible to keep up with the accelerating knowledge development demands of business today. The only options are to do less with the current solutions or to move to alternate methods—one of which is the Web.

In many companies, one of the barriers to this move is, ironically, the Information Technology department. You would think that they would be partners in getting Web learning going; however, often they are not, simply because information technology is such a strategic component of the business that it is in demand on "mission critical" projects—which usually are not about learning. In most companies, even those that hold learning in high esteem, education takes a back seat to most other corporate priorities.

A solution might be to have an external group host your Web learning environment, at least at the beginning. This gives you a way to test and prove that the Web-based solution is effective. If the Information Technology management can see the stability of your solution, and that it is not going to bring down the corporate intranet, they will probably agree to bring it in-house.

A second barrier to Web learning is the baggage of what we did with previous media. In many ways, Web technology does not yet quite deliver the performance required for a compelling learning experience. Instructional designers have not learned how to use the Web effectively, because they are bringing to it design models and metaphors from the paper and classroom days. Once again, we are trying to deliver an existing experience through a new pipe. It takes time to figure out how new technology can deliver new and different experiences, ones where the Web can add value to the current norm.

We need to remember that the Internet was originally designed to facilitate the sharing of knowledge among researchers, and the collaboration that was needed in order to speed innovation. Think about crafting learning experiences to leverage these capabilities for which the Web was designed.

Collaborative Learning Activities

Work gets done through collaboration, and an increasing amount of workplace communication and collaboration happens on the Web. Conversational networks (communities) within your company are where most of the learning happens, where information becomes knowledge and where critical thinking becomes skills (Romiszowski, 1997). Because more and more of these conversations happen on the Web, on-line collaboration itself is a useful skill for your audience to learn and practice. Group learning activities can also help to counteract the isolation and depression that have been found among solitary Web users (Harmon, 1998)—another good reason to not replicate CBT's individual-instruction model (or school's "do you own work" model) in your Web learning environment. Finally, getting your learners together on-line for learning activities might simply be easier than trying to get everyone together in the same room.

Remember, though, that the important element in Web collaboration activities is not the technology but the building of community and relationships so that work can get done. The goal is not collaboration itself, it is the creation of meaning, the sharing of understanding and ideas, and the transmission of knowledge and skills. As the discussion about "communities of learners" in Chapter Four indicated, your learning activities need to be in the context of communities that already exist in your workplace, rather than having learners collaborate just to collaborate.

Real workplace collaborations can be practiced in a Web learning environment, especially if the collaborations already take place on-line because employees are distant from each other in time or space. Examples of practice opportunities that work well on the Web include the following:

Group Writing and Evaluation Projects.   One of the best uses of the Web for a learning activity involves having learners create documents as a team (just like they do at work) and then having managers and experts evaluate them (just like they do at work). Workplace documents are usually the result of a group effort, even if one person did the final write-up. Several departments often get involved.

You can have your learners share ideas in Web discussions or in face-to-face meetings, and then publish their documents on-line. Using HTML and a Web server, learners and experts then edit one document while preserving each person's input. This avoids having to send around numerous paper copies, wait for them to be returned, and then consolidate the changes. The learning can be more immediate, revisions can be produced faster, and the learning that comes from following someone's thought process (through their edits) does not get lost.

Exhibit 8.3 shows the first Web page of a document that several learners have created in HTML and posted to a Web site. (The complete tool is on the Web site.)

Mentoring.   Pairing an expert with a novice can be an exceptional learning experience—for both parties. The problem is that experts in your company are widely scattered and generally very busy. The Web's facilities for open or private discussion and chats means that mentors can provide their perspective and coaching to several people in different locations without having to be present in time or space.

Role-Plays

Up to now, role-plays have been confined to classrooms, under the assumption that human interaction could only really be practiced face to face. However, there are two circumstances in which this may not be true, and where

EXHIBIT 8.3. COLLABORATIVE WRITING AND EVALUATION ACTIVITY TEMPLATE.

This is the first Web page of a document that several learners have created in HTML and posted to a Web site. Experts in the topic have been asked to evaluate the document. The first box (which is yellow on the screen) shows a completed comment. The second yellow box—the one with the scroll bars—shows a comment that has just been typed and is about to be "pasted" (submitted) to the document.

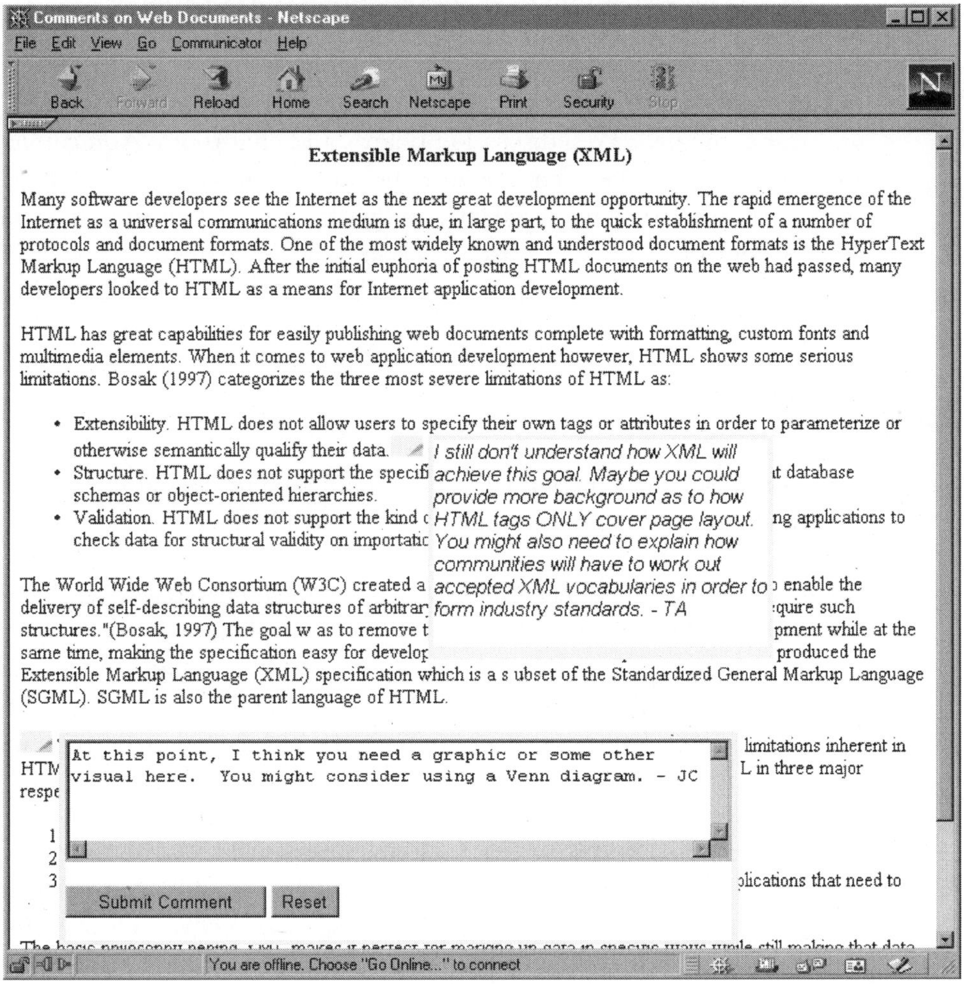

the Web can provide an appropriate practice environment. First, some of your learners may be too intimidated to do live role-playing, at least at the beginning. So instead, show them a model role-play with an HTML script on the Web, and ask them to practice with it in the privacy of their own cubicle. This may be a less frightening first step for some learners than making them start with a conversation with a real person, even if it is "just practice." Second, as Dean Hovey pointed out, many workplace interactions now take place over the Web. You can use MUDs as practice areas for role-playing Web conversations.

For an example of how to do this, see Dean Hovey's Web site at: http://www.pensare.com.

Debates and Problem Solving.   By having your learners join (or "listen in" on) your company's Web discussion boards and chat rooms, you can let them see for themselves what the hot issues are in your company. This will show them what they need to learn and what skills they need to have in order to contribute. Or your learners can start their own discussion by inviting experts or executives to contribute problems or opinions to the learning environment.

Individual Learning Activities

Web activities for the individual learner tend to be those that involve the Tell and Show presentation strategies. They include the following:

Guided Tours.   Individual learners may come to your Web learning environment with different levels of knowledge and skill. Therefore, before putting them into collaborative learning activities, you might want to get everyone to about the same level by offering a guided tour of the content. More advanced learners can skip through it; beginners can use it to get up to speed before they participate in group activities.

Directed Searching and Browsing.   Although they will be collaborating on work projects, your learners often will be responsible for finding information and contacting experts on their own. Learning how to effectively and efficiently search and browse the Web for information that will help them on their jobs is a useful practice activity to put in your Web learning environment.

Asynchronous Response.   Although Web discussion boards involve groups, their asynchronous nature can be used as an individual learning activity. Asynchronous discussions, like e-mail, give learners time to reflect on and plan their responses, and can be a good warm-up to participating in live practice activities and discussions.

Exhibit 8.4 shows a worksheet that you can use to plan the learning activities for your Web learning environment. The worksheet repeats Snyder's four types of learning activities (discovery, invention, production, and generalizing) and includes a column for you to list the group and individual

EXHIBIT 8.4. WEB LEARNING ACTIVITIES WORKSHEET.

Type of Learning Activity	Definition	Web Learning Activities
Discovery	Learners identify the general scope and content of a company's problems and opportunities.	Group Activities: Individual Activities:
Invention	Learners develop ideas and approaches to solveproblems.	Group Activities: Individual Activities:
Production	Learners apply ideas and approaches to meet workplace requirements.	Group Activities: Individual Activities:
Generalizing	Learners document, interpret,and disseminate their competence using groupware, training, apprenticeships, and other transfer methods.	Group Activities: Individual Activities:

activities that your learners will do to practice the content that they have learned.

An Example of Combining Individual and Collaborative Web Learning Activities

Esque (1998, p. 46) reports that he has had success in combining individual and collaborative learning activities in the same Web learning environment. "[We used] the Web to connect the early adopters of new management practices. The simplest application was to collect brief success stories from the users of a specific management practice, and publish those stories on the Web. When training the practices we refer the students to the Web, where they can find recent successful applications from work environments similar to their own. Students are also encouraged to contact early adopters . . . and get some first-hand coaching."

Provide Access to Human Help

In all of your Web learning activities, be sure to give your learners access to an instructor or coach who can help them—not just to canned, textual on-line help. In his efforts to create LearningSpace, a Web-based collaborative learning environment at Lotus Institute, Executive Director Chris Newell discovered how important a human instructor can be in Web learning activities: "We learned that deeper levels of learning happen when [activities] are team-based and instructor-led. . . . For learning to take place, an instructor must be available at the time of need, otherwise there may be a missed opportunity" (Lippincott, 1998, pp. 38–39).

FAST-GLANCE SUMMARY

- Just using the computer may not be enough to get a student to learn the material. Point-and-click is a navigation activity, not a learning activity.

- It may be more important for your learners to know where to find information than to memorize its content. This is the distinction between "knowledge in the world" and "knowledge in the head." It is important for you to decide which knowledge your learners need, and then give them practice activities around it. A useful learning activity is learning where to find information (for example, how to do effective and efficient Web searches).

- Both collaborative and individual learning activities can be done using the Web. One of the best collaborative activities (because it mirrors how work often gets done) is to have a group of learners prepare a document, publish it to the Web, and then have managers and experts comment in real time right on the document.

- Web-based multi-user dialogues or discussions (MUDs) provide a rich conversation environment for learning and practicing human interaction skills. Learners can interact with other people or with simulated characters in a environment resembling an on-line chat room but with more structure and multimedia support.

CHAPTER NINE

ASSESSING WEB LEARNING AND
WEB LEARNING ENVIRONMENTS

OBJECTIVES

After reading this chapter you will be able to

- Explain why the Web may not be an appropriate environment for testing employees.
- Use templates to design assessments that are appropriate for your Web learning environment.
- Explain how the Web can facilitate the delivery of remediation and feedback.

The Problem with Web-Based Testing

This chapter will be brief because, in most cases, the Web is not the right place to test employees' skills. Those skills need to be assessed in real work activities. For example, employees who make products are assessed by the quality or speed with which they make those products. Sales representatives are measured by how many products they sell. Repair technicians' skills are tested according to how fast and how well they repair machines. Managers are assessed by their ability to get others to accomplish tasks. None of these skills can be tested completely by using the Web.

It is true that knowledge tests, such as true-false and multiple-choice, are beginning to be delivered on the Web. It is also true that many professions require knowledge tests, and that Web technology is already making a significant operational contribution to the certification testing business. However, workplace competence is judged by the application of knowledge (that is, by the demonstrated use of skills), and the Web does not add any unique value to knowledge testing itself.

Effective Assessments (Both on and off the Web)

Whether or not your assessments use the Web, they will help learners most if

- The assessment process mirrors how employees are assessed on the job. This does not mean how employees are assessed in their annual performance appraisals, which tend to have many of the same characteristics as knowledge tests. This does mean that assessment is embedded in practice and in real work, not in a separate test.
- You have clearly specified the criteria for competent performance or an acceptable product. Especially in the Web environment, where content can be volatile, your learners will need to know what they must pay attention to and what they can ignore as information changes.

 ॐ ॐ ॐ ॐ ॐ ॐ

This book assumes that your Web learning environment will do more than deliver information. Therefore, traditional knowledge testing is not going to make sense to learners who have been experiencing a collaborative, real-time Web learning environment.

Two questions illustrate why it is difficult to measure collaborative learning on the Web using traditional means:

- How do you assess Web learning when Web content is unbounded and unstable?
- How do you assess collaborative learning?

Measuring Learning When Content Constantly Changes

As preceding chapters have shown, one of the major advantages of using the Web for learning is that it greatly eases the maintenance and update problems of hard copy instructional materials. With the Web, you and your learners and instructors have access to constantly changing information. This means that learners' skills may be more current. But this also means that it may be more difficult for you to freeze their knowledge at any one time so that you can test it. As Hudspeth (1997, p. 355) has noted, "perhaps the most important factor which affects testing is that in a Web-based environment, the content base may change by the nanosecond."

Therefore, knowledge testing by itself probably will not do justice to what your audience has learned in the Web environment. In addition, as you did with learning practice, you will need to plan for learning assessments that mirror how work is actually assessed in your company, which probably is not on the Web.

A Sample Solution

Here is one example of a strategy for having your learners use the Web, but be tested somewhere else. Sales representatives need to know the latest information about your company's products so that they can include it in their sales presentations. To assess their product knowledge, and whether they can apply it to a sales situation, ask your learners to

- Collect product information using the Web.
- Create a presentation collaboratively using Web-based tools.
- Make an in-person presentation to a group of sales managers.

This combined strategy tests the salesperson's ability to use the Web to learn about products, to use Web-based tools to work with colleagues, and to use presentation methods (a non-Web skill) to deliver their sales pitch.

Measuring Collaborative Learning

All the evidence indicates that work—and learning—happens in communities, and that knowing information may actually be less important than knowing how to find information. Nevertheless, the prevailing assessment model, even in highly collaborative industries such as health care, continues to focus on the individual learner and on memorization, that is, on knowledge testing rather than use of skills. Wenger (1996, p. 10) summarizes the problem with using traditional testing methods in collaborative work environments as follows: "We assess learning with tests with which students struggle in a one-on-one combat, where knowledge has to be demonstrated out of context, and where collaborating is cheating." This clearly is not the kind of assessment to which the Web can add anything new, except perhaps a faster delivery medium.

So new assessment models are going to be needed for Web learning environments. These models will evaluate group processes (how well groups worked together) and group outputs (what the group produced). These models will also incorporate both Web and non-Web tests.

A Sample Solution

Because all sales representatives need to use the same basic product presentation, the entire student sales team is evaluated on the quality of the information that they put in the product presentation. A group of senior managers evaluates the content of the presentation, and the whole team of learners is charged with making any necessary changes. Individuals are measured on their ability to deliver the presentation in front of a mock customer panel.

New Methods for Assessing Web Learning

The Web does have some unique contributions to make to a broader conception of assessment, one that does not make such a separation among learning, practice, and work. The field of Web-based assessment is so new that very few examples have yet been created. A few ideas are described below.

Inviting Experts to Evaluate Collaborative Web Work

In the workplace, even if you have the "right answer" (from the knowledge test's perspective), you still need to get others to support your idea. This usually means involving peers, supervisors, and other departments in reviewing your ideas and drafts. A good way to use the Web for learner assessment, then, is to have your learners publish their assignments (such as the sales presentations they created) and invite experts and decision-makers in the company to comment on them and to decide when the learner has "passed" the test. For example, you might have the sales managers make a note when they think that the presentation is ready to give to customers.

This may not feel like the kind of final test that your learners expect from a training program, but it is more like the ongoing assessment of their competence that they will face daily on the job. You could also have learners create documents like the Collaborative Writing and Evaluation Activity Template that you saw in Chapter Eight (Exhibit 8.3) as an assessment device.

Evaluating the Content of Web Discussions

If your learners are participating in a Web discussion or chat as part of the Web learning environment, you can do a content analysis of those forums over time. This type of assessment will show you how your learners' thinking has changed and how they are applying their knowledge and making contributions to the discussion.

For example, if your novice sales representatives have joined a chat room that focuses on how to sell more products to existing customers, you (or a sales manager) might evaluate the suggestions that the novices make to see if they become more frequent or more creative over time.

Connecting Assessments to Learning Resources

In addition to delivering tests, the Web can also contribute to how you give learners their test results. The Web enables you to quickly deliver updated feedback and additional study resources while the learner is still on-line. In traditional courses, you often had to send learners back to the same material, to see if they could learn it a second time. With the Web, you can do that, or you can give learners links to resources that present information in different ways or offer different practice activities.

For example, if you deliver a knowledge test over the Web, you can link each piece of content to an information source that was not part of your original Web learning environment—perhaps the marketing Web site, or an expert technician's e-mail address. When you give learners their test results over the Web, you can show them the items that they missed and attach a list of URLs that contain new resources that specifically address those topics. The learners can then link immediately to those resources while the context of the missed items is still fresh in their minds.

Exhibit 9.1 shows the opening Web page of a template that you can use for returning feedback and linked resources to learners when they have completed a test. Links take learners back to the course materials or out to other resources that they can use to enhance their knowledge and skills. Also notice that the feedback form uses some system statistics (such as this learner's seventy-six-day lapse between taking two of the courses) that can be used to help the learner understand the need for more frequent training.

Using the Web for Individual Self-Assessment

The same feedback-with-resources strategy works well for Web-based self-assessments. If employees (or their supervisors) take an on-line self-assessment, the areas for development can be returned with a list of Web-based resources that employees can use to develop their skills and knowledge. The list of resources can be updated and an automatic e-mail message can be sent to learners when new material is available. You can use the following three tools to create Web-based self-assessments for your learners.

Exhibit 9.2 shows the opening Web page of a template for conducting self-assessments over the Web, and Exhibit 9.3 shows a template for returning the results of the self-assessment to the learners. Employees, and perhaps their supervisors, would complete the assessment by selecting the radio buttons that match the employees' development needs. They would then receive tailored feedback designed to help with the needs identified in the self-assessment.

EXHIBIT 9.1. ASSESSMENT FEEDBACK
AND RESOURCES TEMPLATE.

This is the opening Web page of a template that you can use for returning feedback and linked resources to learners when they have completed a test. Points to notice:

- Courses to be repeated or reviewed are presented as links. This makes it easy for the learner to get back to the material.

- System statistics are reported in Tips designed to help the learner understand the need for additional work.

Computer Repair Feeback Suggestions - Inbox - Netscape Folder

File Edit View Go Message Communicator Help

Get Msg New Msg Reply Reply All Forward File Next Print Delete Stop

Subject	Sender	Date
Online learning material change notification	Thor Anderson	8:17 PM
Computer Repair Feeback Suggestions	Thor Anderson	11:01 PM

Dear Samantha,

Our custom feedback engine has reviewed your scores for the "Computer Repair 101" series of courses you recently completed. We congratulate you on the successful completion of 14 out of the 16 courses in the series. There are, however, a few courses we think you may wish to revisit. Based upon a thorough review of your performance, we make the following suggestions:

Courses that should be taken over again:

Course Title - "CPU Troubleshooting and Replacement"
Reason: Your total score of 67 out of a possible 100 is not sufficient to pass this course.

Tips: You may not have spent as much time on this topic as is needed. Compared to the other courses where you averaged 1.65 hours per course, you only required 45 minutes for this course.

Course Title - "Diagnosing Video Card Problems"
Reason: Your total score of 28 out of a possible 38 is a passing grade, but is lower than your average score for the other courses you have completed.

Tips: Our records indicate a period of 76 days between when you took the Video Card Architecture course and the Diagnosing Video Card Problems course. You may wish to review the course "Video Card Architecture", which you performed well on, before taking the diagnosing course again. Many of the principles explained in the architecture course are relevant to the course on diagnosing problems.

You may re-enroll in any of these courses by selecting them.

Kind regards,

Online Learning Staff

Total messages: 203   Unread messages: 0

EXHIBIT 9.2. SELF-ASSESSMENT TEMPLATE.

This is the opening Web page of a site designed to allow learners to conduct self-assessments over the Web.

Acme Skills Assessment Page - Netscape

File   Edit   View   Go   Communicator   Help

Back   Forward   Reload   Home   Search   Netscape   Print   Security   Stop   N

Bookmarks   Go to: http://acme.skillassess.com/   What's Related

Acme Corporation Job Skill Assessment

1.   I enjoy solving problems on my own.
- ○   A. Strongly Agree
- ○   B. Somewhat Agree
- ○   C. Somewhat Disagree
- ○   D. Strongly Disagree

2.   I prefer a job where I can learn a correct sequence or procedure and then do it consistently over and over again.
- ○   A. Strongly Agree
- ○   B. Somewhat Agree
- ○   C. Somewhat Disagree
- ○   D. Strongly Disagree

3.   When I work, I like to just "get things done" instead of worrying too much about scheduling my time.
- ○   A. Strongly Agree
- ○   B. Somewhat Agree
- ○   C. Somewhat Disagree
- ○   D. Strongly Disagree

4.   I adapt easily when working with people from different cultures and backgrounds.
- ○   A. Strongly Agree
- ○   B. Somewhat Agree

You are offline. Choose "Go Online.." to c

EXHIBIT 9.3. SELF-ASSESSMENT FEEDBACK AND RESOURCES TEMPLATE.

This Web page returns the results of the self-assessment to the learners. The items in the self-assessment are linked to learning resources, and different resources are suggested depending on how the learner scores on the self-assessment. In this sample, the employee needs development most in time management and people management. At the bottom of the page, two learning resources are recommended to help the employee develop in those areas.

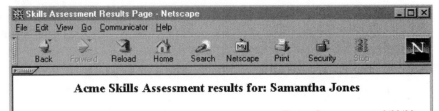

Acme Skills Assessment results for: Samantha Jones

Date of assessment: 2/22/99

SCORE:
Your overall score is 36 out of 50. This suggests that you have an aptitude for managing people, but should consider taking some courses to sharpen your managerial skills. Category results are listed below. Course suggestions are provided at the bottom of this document.

Basic Management Skills	4 of 4
Time Management	4 of 6
Managing Groups and Teams	6 of 10
Dealing with Budgets	7 of 8
Motivating Employees	5 of 6
Task Management	5 of 5
Advanced Managing Skills	5 of 8

Total Score 36/50

Your scores show a solid knowledge of entry level Management. Picking up some specific training on managing groups and teams will help you. You will also benefit from a review of advanced Managing skills. Combined with what you already know, these additional courses will give you the tools to advance toward the "Intermediate" manager level within Acme.

Suggested Courses: (click on course name to enroll)

Team Management - offered by ManagePro Inc.

Advanced Corporate Management - offered by ManagePro Inc.

Exhibit 9.4 shows an e-mail message template that you can use to notify learners when new resources become available. The first section of the template links to resources based on the employee's self-assessment profile. The second section of the template alerts the employee to new topics and links to resources that pertain to them.

Evaluating the Web Learning Environment

In addition to testing your learners to ensure that they got the skills they needed, you also may want to evaluate your Web learning environment itself. If tests show that your learners did not get the skills they needed, it may not be the learners that need help. Perhaps they had trouble with the technology, or perhaps they did well for a while until the novelty of Web learning wore off and it became a disruption of their normal work routine.

Assessing learning includes assessing the learning environment. Here are some ways of evaluating your Web learning site:

- Evaluating one proposed lesson before the whole learning environment is built. This will tell you whether or not the technology and the content will work for your learners (Driscoll, 1998).
- Assessing how your learners are using the site by analyzing system logs to see the following data, which will show you if learners are using the Web site as you intended:
  Volume of activity (how many learners visit the site)
  Paths that learners take through the site
  Time that learners spend on the site (Ravitz, 1997)
- Giving learners the opportunity to send you feedback on how the technology works (or not), on the content and how it is organized and presented, and on the learning activities. For example, feedback buttons, Web-based surveys, and links that generate automatic e-mail messages can help to establish an effective line of communication between the learner and the Web learning designer for ongoing assessment of the environment.

EXHIBIT 9.4. LEARNING RESOURCE UPDATE TEMPLATE.

This illustrates the format of an e-mail message that you can use to notify learners of appropriate resources. The letter offers two types of resources:

- Links to resources based on the employee's self-assessment profile.
- Links to new topics and resources that pertain to them.

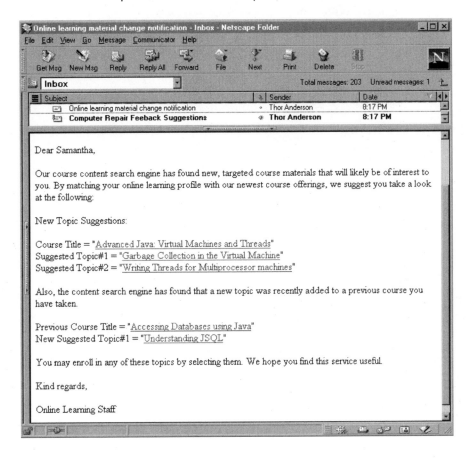

EXHIBIT 9.5. WEB LEARNING FEEDBACK TEMPLATE.

This is the opening page of a questionnaire that allows people to inform the Web learning designer of what works or does not work about a specific course. Note use of the various elements for different purposes:

- Check boxes to facilitate replies where several answers may be true at once
- Radio buttons for replies where only one response can be true at a time
- Text boxes for open-ended replies
- Status bar message (at the bottom of the screen) to keep the learner oriented and explain the behavior of the site

Exhibit 9.5 shows the opening page of a template for gathering learners' feedback about the Web learning environment. This chapter's "To Learn More About" section contains a resource on how to evaluate learning environments.

FAST-GLANCE SUMMARY

- The Web is not "good" or "bad" for any particular kind of assessment. All tests, whether Web-based or not, need to reflect the tasks that employees actually do on the job.
- You can assess Web learning in the following ways:
  —Have experts comment on group learning projects, either by annotating them on-line or by posting their comments to discussion boards.
  —Analyze the content of learners' on-line discussions, to determine how they are thinking and learning about the topic.
  —Have learners create their own assessments of their Web learning.
- Web technology makes a significant contribution to delivering timely feedback and resources to learners.
- You can attach URLs to test or self-assessment results and send them to learners so that they will have easy access to resources. You can also send automatic e-mail alerts with URLs when new resources become available on topics that learners have been studying.

To Learn More About ...

Evaluating learning environments:
Beer, V., & Bloomer, A. C. (1986). Levels of evaluation. *Educational Evaluation and Policy Analysis, 8*(4), 335–346.

Skill assessment software:
Auerbach, S. (1997, July/August). Mining for skills. *Inside Technology Training,* pp. 40–53.

Software for creating Web-delivered knowledge tests:
See Appendix A at the end of this book.

CHAPTER TEN

USING INSTRUCTORS IN WEB LEARNING ENVIRONMENTS

OBJECTIVES

After reading this chapter you will be able to
- Explain the benefits of using the Web as a resource for instructors in traditional classrooms.
- Describe the skills needed by instructors in virtual Web classrooms.
- Create an Instructor Guide for your Web learning instructors.

The Web and the Instructor

Instructors have new roles to play when the Web is part of a learning environment. They may no longer need to be the deliverers of factual information. However, instructors are still needed to help Web learners with several tasks:

- Navigate Web resources.
- Learn collaboratively (perhaps without ever meeting face to face).
- Create meaning and develop skills from an overwhelming amount of information.

Instructors are as important as ever when the learning environment includes the Web, and "doing away with the human contact would be disastrous" (Young, 1997, p. 3, quoting Mary Bergan, general secretary of the American Association of University Professors). Web learners need help to create knowledge from the Web's vast amount of information.

This chapter looks at two new possibilities that have opened up for the classroom instructor with the advent of the Web:

- Using the Web as a resource for a traditional classroom course, either in the classroom or as an outside or post-training resource.
- Using the Web as a "virtual classroom" that contains many of the elements of traditional classrooms (such as lectures, exercises, homework, tests) but where the learners are not together physically.

The Web in the Traditional Classroom

The traditional classroom has been largely ignored in the rush to get learning materials to the Web, but the use of the Web as an in-class resource can make a substantial contribution to learning. Keeping your company's instructors current on new developments, such as new products, is a very expensive and time-consuming activity. However, by using the Web as an in-class resource, your instructors can have the latest information at their fingertips. (This is another application of the "knowledge in the world" versus "knowledge in the head" principle introduced in Chapter Eight.) If your instructors know where to find the knowledge in the world, such as on a Web site that was created for their class, then they do not need to keep so much soon-outdated knowledge in their heads. They can concentrate on helping their learners instead.

A Web site for your company's product training instructors can give them the latest product information without the time and expense of taking them out of class for their own refresher training. The in-class Web site could contain instructor notes and slides, lab or activity directions, and links to other resources such as competitors' Web sites. In addition, you would be updating all the information from a central source—the Web server—so that the instructors and the learners always had the latest product information.

If you expanded your instructors' Web site to take advantage of its collaborative features, your classroom instructors worldwide could instantly share teaching tips and the latest information through instructors' news groups, chat rooms, or Web-based "teachers' lounges."

Uses for the Web in Traditional Classrooms

- Source of updated content
- Repository for slides, lecture notes, and assignments that can be accessed anytime
- Links to supplemental material on other sites
- Topical discussions moderated by instructor
- Chat room for learners to discuss content and assignments
- "Teachers' lounge" where instructors can share ideas with each other
- Collaborative space for learners to publish or work on projects together electronically

꧁ ꧁ ꧁ ꧁ ꧁ ꧁

The Web as a Virtual Classroom

In addition to using the Web in traditional brick-and-mortar classrooms, you and your instructors may want to use Web technologies to create "virtual classrooms."

Creating Virtual Classrooms

The tools needed to build virtual classrooms are complex, and cannot readily be shown in print. However, several commercial tools for creating synchronous and asynchronous Web classrooms are listed in Appendix A at the end of the book.

꧁ ꧁ ꧁ ꧁ ꧁ ꧁

These are some of the characteristics common among virtual classrooms:

- Classes convene at learners' desktops or laptops.
- Instructors "lecture" from notes that everyone can access.

- Instructors and learners draw on shared (electronic) whiteboards. (For a demonstration of electronic whiteboards, go to http://www.placeware.com.)
- Learners collaborate on group projects, perhaps without ever meeting face to face.
- Learners and instructors communicate with each other using chat rooms, discussion boards, and e-mail between classes.
- Instructors and learners collaboratively assess projects, homework assignments, and tests that are posted to the Web site.

The Role of the Instructor in a Virtual Classroom

This option to hold class on the Web sounds exciting, and has the immediate promise of being able to make your instructors available across time and space. However, many of your company's instructors may be subject-matter experts, not educators. Their teaching skills may be adequate for a classroom in which lecture is the major activity and questions can be asked directly, but may not be up to teaching or helping learners in a virtual Web classroom.

Exhibit 10.1 lists eight skills for the instructor in a virtual classroom. Use this list with instructors who are now subject-matter experts to educate them about what they will need to do differently to facilitate Web learning.

Web teaching is less about information dissemination and more about organizing the students' interaction with each other and the material, and this requires the instructor to be responsive and competent in on-line activity. (See Shotsberger, 1997, for an interesting discussion of this aspect of the job.) In her research on instructor effectiveness in virtual Web classrooms, Hiltz (1995, p. 8) found that Web learning instructors needed to have skills in instructional design and collaboration management, and that "the single most important behavioral practice which produces relatively good results in online courses is the timely and 'personal' (in tone) response by instructors to questions and contributions of students online."

In this chapter's "Lessons from the Field" interview, Steve Zahm from DigitalThink talks about what it takes to recruit, train, and manage instructors in virtual classrooms.

EXHIBIT 10.1. EIGHT SKILLS FOR THE SUCCESSFUL WEB INSTRUCTOR.

Because virtual classroom teaching and management may be new to many instructors, Hiltz (1995) offers the following guidelines for how to be an instructor in a Web learning environment:

1. *Watch your use of language closely.* Learners may not have any clues, such as tone or body language, that they have in a real classroom. In particular, be careful about using ALL CAPITAL LETTERS—it can be interpreted as shouting.

2. *Keep Web lectures short.* Break up lectures with opportunities for learners to participate and contribute their knowledge and experience. Open up a discussion or invite contributions to an electronic whiteboard.

3. *Constantly help learners to participate.* Ask questions of individual learners, and call on other learners to answer. Praise learners who contribute content. Grade learners on the quality of their contributions as well as on their test or project scores.

4. *Assign work that requires collaboration.* Make learners contact experts or other learners to find information.

5. *Schedule—and keep—on-line office hours.* Let learners know when you will be on-line so they will not become frustrated while they wait for a response from you.

6. *Provide a syllabus.* Post a schedule of lectures, lessons, and assignment due dates on the Web site. Be consistent about posting new material.

7. *Provide frequent summaries and reviews.* This will help everyone keep up with the material.

8. *Keep the class size between ten and thirty learners.* You need enough participants for collaboration, but not so many that the instructor is overwhelmed by the amount of posting, responding, and evaluating, or by having to moderate too many discussions.

LESSONS FROM THE FIELD

Using Instructors in Web Learning Environments

Steve Zahm is a founder and vice-president of marketing for DigitalThink
(http://www.digitalthink.com), which offers Web-based technology training
courses for programmers, developers, system administrators, and end users.
As part of its Web learning environment, DigitalThink uses instructors to provide asynchronous support to learners.

KEY POINTS

Zahm's Key Points About Using Instructors in Web Learning

- Learners need to interact with instructors, even in a self-paced learning
  environment.
- Instructors play an important role in initiating and guiding Web discussions.
- Instructors need guidance on how to customize their teaching (and not
  just the content) for different types of learners in the global Web learning
  environment.

How to Recruit, Train, and Manage Instructors
in a Global Web Learning Environment

Zahm: It is backwards to think that we can remove humans from the learning equation. One of the great lessons of self-paced CD-ROM training was
that learners still needed a human somewhere to answer questions and provide guidance.

　　We recruit instructors from on-line sources and from our existing student
base. They have to demonstrate mastery of the course material, in addition
to having a formal education or certification in the topic. When those criteria
are met, we put them through an on-line course on how to be an on-line instructor. After that, we assign them to a mentor program in which they are
paired with one of our experienced instructors. New instructors copy their

mentor on all their e-mail, so that the mentor can audit the response to make sure it is accurate.

All of our instructor interaction happens through e-mail. When students submit an exercise, they immediately receive an automated response; immediate response is very important for adult learners. A few hours later, they also receive a personal note from their instructor with a specific critique of their exercise. All exercises are graded by an instructor, since the subject matter (such as network installation) can be very open-ended and unique to each situation.

Instructors are measured by the quality and speed of their response. The average time to respond to a learner's inquiry is eight and a half to nine hours. Instructors can work full time or part time, and they are scheduled by an operations group that assigns office hours for them.

How Learners and Instructors Interact and Collaborate on the Web

Zahm: We have learned that on-line collaboration does not work if it is forced, or if the issue is not one that people need to discuss. (Topics such as "How can you implement spell check in a word processing program?" don't have enough gray area to be worth interacting about.) We have also learned that people are not yet familiar with the "discussion" metaphor in an on-line environment.

What works is when the instructors initiate much of the discussion in the beginning. Controversial topics are a good way to get the conversation started. The instructor can then participate less once people are engaged.

We have also learned that asynchronous discussions are more valuable than scheduled, synchronous ones. Not everyone is ready to talk or be trained at the same time, so it is better to allow them to participate when they are ready.

Important Considerations for Building and Distributing Web Learning Globally

Zahm: Here are the most important things to remember:

- In addition to localizing the content, you also need to "localize" the instructors so that they can be sensitive to different learning styles in different cultures.

- If you keep your training within the Web browser, you will have fewer problems with differences in computer platforms.
- Speed is a consideration; build for the lowest common platform. The lower the bandwidth, the better.
- Home Web users in many countries are charged by the minute for Internet access. Since many employees take their training at home, it is important to know what the home computer configurations are.

Advice for Making the Learning-Versus-Technology Argument

Zahm: It is important to look at the goal. The assumption that executives make is that a well-trained employee force is a strategic advantage. So they want to deliver more of a good thing, that is, training. The problem is that they focus on the delivery mechanism. They went running down the CD-ROM road, and now they want to do the same thing with the Web.

But training is not about delivering content, it is about creating knowledge and about tracking learning. Trainers need to position themselves as experts in how people learn, not as experts in technology or production. They need to concentrate on learning, not on how fast they can get content out there.

Web learning allows for rapid content changes and student tracking on a scale that just cannot be done in other media. But it is not about the bells and whistles. It is about understanding how people learn. Training professionals need to ask, What is the goal? and then ask, How can the technology help?

Web-Based Instructor Support

Whether your instructors are teaching in a real or virtual classroom, you will need to create an Instructor Guide to support them in their use of the Web as a learning tool. Instructors can then establish separate Web sites designed for each class that include links to material from the guide as well as areas designed for interaction. Instructor Guides can include everything an instructor needs to teach a course:

- Lecture notes
- Slides or other graphical materials
- Descriptions of exercises and labs
- Assignments for learners
- Tests
- Criteria for grading assignments and tests
- Lists of equipment or materials needed for the class

You may also need to create a Student Guide for your learners that contains assignments, schedules, and other information. Both guides should be accessible on the Web. Both can be created from one source—the Web Instructor Guide. Because the Web-based information and URLs that will be in the guides will change frequently, it will be easier for you to maintain and update both guides if they are based on one source. That way, you can simply extract the relevant sections for the Student Guide, and know that it will be synchronized with the Instructor Guide. In addition, having one guide reinforces organizational learning and the idea that learners can contribute directly to the curriculum; they (and the instructors) simply make changes to one guide that everyone in the class can then access.

The contents for a Web Instructor Guide are outlined below, and apply to traditional classrooms that are using the Web or to virtual classrooms.

Web Instructor Guide

The Web site for your traditional or virtual classroom should contain seven elements; how you arrange them will depend on such factors as the amount of content and how your instructor prefers to use the Web site.

Course Overview and Objectives.   This gives your learners an idea of what they will be able to do when they have finished using the learning environment. This should appear on the guide's home page.

Content Outlines and Instructor Lecture Notes.   This is a good place to use links. Rather than putting all of the notes with the outline in one long page, "chunk" the notes so that they link from the various sections of the outline. This gives you (and the instructor) the advantage of being able to more easily cross-reference different sections of content by linking various URLs. It also makes for less scrolling by the instructor during a lecture. The lecture notes should be in bullet form instead of narrative, so that the instructor can run through the content quickly and customize the details for the particular class. These bullets themselves could be links that jump to references, more detailed information, or class activities.

Learner Activities and Assessments. This section includes directions, materials, grading criteria, time allotments, lists of experts who may be contacted, and any other information for learners regarding projects that they will be doing to practice the skills that they are learning. Be sure to include directions for how and where the assignments should be turned in or published (if the product is a Web document). If your instructors are new to managing virtual classrooms, you may want to give specific guidelines on how to moderate discussions and chat groups and how to manage virtual collaboration among learners. If tests are to be administered, include guidelines for how (and if) learners may collaborate or use non-class resources, and what the time limit is for the test.

Media Requirements and Directions. Part of your Web learning environment may involve media elements such as video or audio, which may or may not be played on the Web. Link the media pieces (or the directions for using non-Web pieces) directly from the related sections in the content outline or lecture notes. This will keep your instructor from having to search for the right media element in the middle of a lecture. Include the following in the directions:

- Objectives for the media piece (what the learner should be able to do because of it)
- Key points for the instructor to use in a summary
- Directions for using the equipment (or the Web control panel)
- Plug-ins or other applications that may need to be downloaded or installed before the media can be played
- Time length of the piece

In addition, if the media element is one that the instructor presents, you will need to indicate where the instructor should pause for discussion or questions.

Approximate Timing.   Let the instructor and learners know how long they should expect to work on each content section so that they can fit the learning into their workday (or know how much after-hours time they will need to spend). Hiltz (1995, p. 6) emphasizes the importance of keeping the Web class at least somewhat together in time so that the discussions and collaborations will be synchronized: "The medium is self-paced in the sense that each student can read and write at their own pace; however, the class has to move through the modules together, in order for interaction to be meaningful."

List of Learning Materials.   Because the Web may be only one part of your company's learning environment, let instructors and learners know what else is required so that they will have all materials at hand while they are learning.

Tips on How to Help Learners.   In both traditional and virtual classrooms, having the Web as the factual resource frees the instructor to help learners go beyond the facts and form a community to solve real workplace problems. To support your instructors in their roles as guides and moderators, include the following in your Web Instructor Guide:

- Questions that learners are likely to ask, with links to sources of updated answers
- Suggestions for dealing with novice and advanced learners in the same class, with links to advanced or remedial material and with recommendations for how advanced learners can add their knowledge to the curriculum, or how they can serve as chat or discussion moderators
- Suggestions for dealing with novice and advanced Web users in the same class, including links to tutorials on how to use the Web and recommendations to give learners about how to behave in Web interactions
- Recommendations for advanced (or remedial) assignments or activities for learners who finish early (or late)
- Common errors that learners are likely to make, including suggestions for helping them recover from the error (suggestions such as sending a question via e-mail to an "expert" in their work area, or posting their problem to a discussion board)
- Suggestions for what to do if the class is significantly behind or ahead of schedule, including which sections can be condensed or omitted and what additional material might be delivered if there is time

EXHIBIT 10.2. INSTRUCTOR WEB SITE TEMPLATE.

This is the opening page of a class Web site. Note the following major elements:

- Course topic outline in the upper left frame. Each topic is a live link to notes and presentation materials.

- Related resource links in the lower left frame.

- Display area for the slides or other presentation materials in the large central pane.

- Interactive area where learners—who have the same Web site up on their computers—can submit questions directly to the instructor's computer via the scrolling text block at the bottom. The instructor's presentation can then be modified to reflect the answers. With most Web software, questions can be directed either to the instructor alone or to the whole list. The learner or the instructor (or both) can control this.

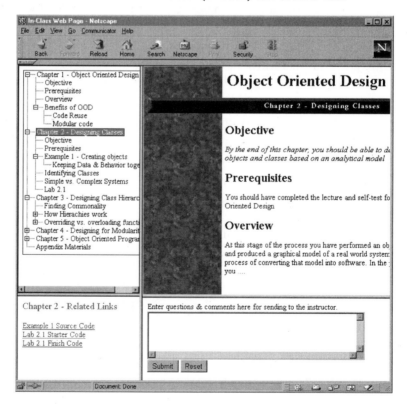

- Additional resources and contacts that can be referenced if a learner presses for more information or is not satisfied with the instructor's answer
- Recommendations for alternative procedures if the network goes down or if non-Web equipment fails

Because of the speed with which Web information changes, you will also need to have a system for letting the instructor and the learner know when any of the material in the guide has changed. You might develop an e-mail notification procedure to use when new material becomes available. In addition to simply announcing the changes, tell instructors and learners if the material is new, if it replaces old material, or if it supplements existing material. Be specific about what they need to do with it: is it "need to know" information that will require them to change a skill, or is it "nice to know" reference material?

Instructor's Web Site

Each class taught on or supported by material on the Web will benefit from having its own Web site. The instructor can provide links to the course outline and resources, and support the level of interaction needed for the class. Exhibit 10.2 shows the opening page of a Web site for a classroom instructor who is teaching on the Web. It provides a mechanism for learners to ask questions while the course is in progress, allowing the instructor to incorporate the answers into the presentation so that all the learners in the class can benefit from the information and insight that develops as a result of each one's participation.

FAST-GLANCE SUMMARY

- Instructors have a new role to play in Web learning environments; they need to help learners make sense of the overwhelming amount of information on the Web and use Web technology to learn collaboratively.
- An in-class Web site can provide the latest information so that instructors do not have to be taken out of class so often for refresher training.
- Teaching in synchronous or asynchronous Web classrooms may be a new experience for your instructors. Creating a Web Instructor Guide, and

including tips for managing on-line discussions and collaborative learning activities, will help your instructors teach with or on the Web.

To Learn More About ...

Processes and criteria for instructor-developed software:

Hanley, G. L., Schneebeck, C., & Zweier, L. (1998). *Implementing a scalable and sustainable model for instructional software development.* Long Beach: California State University, http://www.cdl.edu/html/syllabus98.html.

Web resources for instructors (primarily K–12):

Hackbarth, S. (1997). Web-based learning activities for children. In B. Khan (Ed.), *Web-based instruction* (pp. 191–212). Englewood Cliffs, NJ: Educational Technology Publications.

A SUMMARY OF LEARNING AND TECHNICAL CONSIDERATIONS FOR WEB LEARNING ENVIRONMENTS

OBJECTIVE

After reading this chapter you will be able to
- Design a Web environment that includes characteristics that support learning.

Requirements for an Effective Web Learning Environment

The purpose of this final chapter is to summarize all the suggestions that have been made throughout this book on how to design a Web learning environment. As you use the tools, templates, and worksheets that have been provided in this book to put together your Web learning environment, you might want to keep in mind four lessons that the creators of one of the largest Web-based training environments, the Microsoft On Line Institute (MOLI, http://www.microsoft.com/train_cert/), discovered (Rose, 1998):

1. Instructional design is a must; people do not learn from just another pretty site.
2. It matters what computer equipment you and your learners have, and it takes a considerable amount of that equipment to develop and deliver Web learning.

3. People do not like to read on-line; they need short pages, and they want to be able to print them.
4. Chats and discussions need to be focused and moderated or they quickly get off-track.

In creating a Web learning site for training and human performance technology professionals, Rossett and her team learned the following lessons about Web learning design (Rossett, Keenan, and Adgate, 1997, pp. 24–25):

- Design for the lowest common platform.
- Use a few simple graphics.
- Test on different platforms.
- Simplify the story line (think in terms of screens, not pages or binders).
- Incorporate more interactivity.
- Plan for maintenance and continuity.

As these lessons indicate, both learning and technical considerations are important as you put your Web learning environment together.

Learning Considerations

The first point in the MOLI list—that instructional design is more important than a pretty Web site—is crucial to the success of your Web learning environment. Regardless of the media and delivery vehicles that you have chosen, make sure you address the ten questions in Exhibit 11.1—they will help you remember that learning, not glitz, is the goal. Use this list after you've drafted your learning Web site but before you go to final production to make sure that your site is focused on learning.

Technical and Web Considerations

Once you have put the learning elements together, you can put the technical elements of your Web environment in place. Hanley, Schneebeck, and Zweier (1998, p. 4) suggest four considerations for using any technology (including the Web) for learning:

EXHIBIT 11.1. A CHECKLIST OF
LEARNING CONSIDERATIONS FOR WEB SITES.

1. Because this is a workplace environment focused on skills development (and not on casual browsing and incidental learning), are there specific objectives that let learners know what they will be able to do as a result of the instruction?

2. Is there content for each objective?

3. Do any of the media, materials, and methods of presentation distract from or conflict with the learning experience?

4. Have the materials been designed to support both learning and performance support, in case the user needs to find out what to do but does not have time to practice and internalize the skill just now?

5. Does the navigation show the following cues:
   • Where the learner is and what comes next?
   • The progress made so far and how much remains?
   • How to get out, home, or back to a familiar point?
   • What the learner is supposed to do at the destination link?

6. Is there evidence of a consistent instructional strategy in the way that content and other elements are displayed and organized, and in the way that learners are asked to interact with the content?

7. Do the learning activities and test items
   • Mirror the performance stated in the objective?
   • Provide useful feedback and help the learner undo erroneous thinking (rather than just saying that their answer was right or wrong)?
   • Refer the learner back to the content or to other resources?
   • Bridge to real practice and activities (if the courseware does not offer those)?

8. Is single-learner instruction enhanced wherever possible by activities that build the learning community, such as group exercises and other collaborative activities?

9. Is the learner given a time limit or estimated time to complete the courseware?

10. Are materials that are not included with the courseware, but that the learner will need, listed up front so that the learner can arrange for a complete environment?

1. Effectiveness of the technology to achieve the users' goals. (Is the Web the right medium for what your learners need?)
2. Ease of learning to use the technology by new users. (Do your learners need to learn how to use the Web before they can learn from it?)
3. Ease of using the technology by trained users. (Will expert Web users be tempted to critique your Web site rather than learn from it?)
4. Preference for using the technology. (Do your learners want to learn this way?)

For the Web specifically, there are myriad considerations that will either ensure or block any learning that you hoped would happen from your Web site. Several references at the end of this chapter contain lists of what to avoid and what to do when using the Web in general. Exhibit 11.2 contains a checklist of dos and don'ts designed to ensure that your use of Web technology will promote learning. Remembering to ask yourself, "What do my learners need to learn?" before "How can I use the Web to teach them?" can help you avoid many of the technical pitfalls of the Web.

Test, Test, Test . . . and Test Again

After you have put your learning Web site all together, you will need to test your Web learning environment thoroughly before it goes live. You will need to run tests with a whole range of factors:

- Learners who have different learning styles, to make sure that a broad audience can get the skills they need from a Web experience
- Learners who have different levels of experience and comfort with the technology, to make sure that the equipment does not get in the way of the learning or that an errant mouse click will not crash the system
- Every possible hardware and software configuration that your learners are likely to have, including diverse hardware platforms, operating systems (including different versions of the same operating system), and Web browsers (including different versions of the same browser)
- Local, remote, and off-line learners to make sure that the learning experience does not degrade with distance and slower networks

EXHIBIT 11.2. A CHECKLIST OF TECHNICAL DOS AND DON'TS FOR WEB LEARNING ENVIRONMENTS.

This checklist asks you to make sure that you *did* use some of the technical features of the Web to promote learning, and *did not* make any of the technical errors that are common to poorly designed Web sites.

DOs: My learning Web site

☐ Does reflect an instructional design strategy. I created a "learning specification" (in addition to the technical specification), and I stuck to it. If the technology did not fit the learning specification, I changed to a different technology.

☐ Does involve the learners right away, and gives them a way to interact with and contribute their expertise to the learning environment by using the Web's collaborative tools.

☐ Does show a map or other device so that the learner is never lost in Web space.

☐ Does include an "escape hatch" (such as e-mail) to a real human being who can answer content questions and give guidance on technical problems.

☐ Does allow printing, if the learner wants a hard copy.

☐ Does contain links that work.

☐ Does have flexibility for the future, so that the site is both easy to maintain and flexible enough to accept new instructional approaches and content, without suffering radical changes in look and feel.

DON'Ts: My learning Web site

☐ Does not use unnecessary multimedia.

☐ Does not use the Web as just a self-paced learning environment without tapping its capacity for enabling collaborative learning. (In fact, research from Carnegie-Mellon University makes a strong case for not using the Web as a self-paced learning environment because of the isolation and depression that can result from solitary Web use [Harmon, 1998]).

☐ Does not use distracting elements such as blink tags, marquees, or rotating banners.

(continued on next page)

EXHIBIT 11.2. *(continued)*

☐ Does not leave the learner stuck on a page without an obvious way to get out or back to a familiar place.

☐ Does not have links that go nowhere, or that return a "file not found" error message.

☐ Does not make learners wait for long downloads (especially without a progress indicator).

Seven Sites Created with Learning in Mind

There are undoubtedly many excellent workplace Web learning sites; unfortunately, most of them are behind corporate firewalls where you cannot access them. The following seven examples are of free, public sites that exemplify the principles of Web learning that you have learned in this book. Take a look at them and see what you might incorporate from them in your own Web learning environments. Use the worksheet from Chapter Two (Exhibit 2.1) to make notes about how these sites promote learning.

Delivery Sites

Center for Distributed Learning
http://www.cdl.edu
What to notice:

- Interactive simulations and labs that do not require plug-ins
- Text and simulations side by side

Hotwired (On-Line Version of Wired Magazine)
http://www.hotwired.com/Webmonkey/
What to notice:

- Compact content, with minimal page scrolling
- Model-based practice (compare your work to the model)

- Rotating graphics and busy border (a negative example—note the distraction factor as something to avoid)

Pan Media
http://learn2.com
What to notice:

- Compact, task-based content
- Helpful graphics that do not require plug-ins

PBS Nova Program: The Pyramids
http://www.pbs.org/wgbh/pages/nova/pyramid
What to notice:

- Use of pictures and maps for navigation
- Graphic resolution quality (high, low, or photographic) selectable by user

Catalog Site

New Promise
http://www.caso.com
What to notice:

- Course index that can be searched in a variety of ways
- Good example of a "portal site" (a site that leads to other sites), which may be useful if you are planning a large Web learning environment

Resource Sites

Access Excellence (Genentech)
http://www.gene.com/ae
What to notice:

- Excellent example of a Web site for classroom instructors
- Table of contents that has text sections that do not change (such as What's New, Activities Exchange) next to graphics that link to specific topics that do change periodically
- Learning activities contributed by instructors
- Access to experts (Access Excellence Fellows)

- On-line collaborative projects
- Moderated, threaded discussions

Alberta (Canada) Education
http://ednet.edc.gov.ab.ca
What to notice:

- Multilingual and multicultural versions of the site
- Features that cater to multiple education audiences
- Excellent example of an easy-to-use site map
- Unobtrusive, persistent navigational frame

FAST-GLANCE SUMMARY

- Focus on learning first, and then apply the Web's technologies to helping your learners get the information and skills they need.
- Test your Web site with learners all through the development process, to make sure that they can use the site as you intended.

To Learn More About . . .

Creating your Web site's architecture and user interface:
Berst, J. (1998, October 8). Don't make this Web site mistake. ZDNet Anchor Desk—for the general site: http://www.zdnet.com/anchordesk; for this specific article: http://www.zdnet.com/anchordesk/story_index_19981008.html.

Building a better interface—complete list of tips and picks:
C|Net Builder.com—http://www.builder.com.
Dynamic Diagrams, Inc.—http://www.dynamicdiagrams.com.

Tools and seminars for Web site architecture and mapping:
Dyroweb—http://www.dyrowebic/wbt/index.html.

Guidelines and examples for creating Web-based training:
Flanders, V., & Willis, M. (1996). *Web pages that suck.* San Francisco: Sybex.
Jones, M. G., and Farquhar, J. D. (1997). User interface design for Web-

based instruction. In B. Khan (Ed.), *Web-based instruction* (pp. 239–244). Englewood Cliffs, NJ: Educational Technology Publications.

Nielsen, J. (1996, May). Top ten mistakes in Web design. Sun Microsystems Alert Box—http://www.sun.com/960416/columns/alertbox/ index.html; see also Jakob Nielsen's user interface design site—http://www.useit.com/alertbox.

Rosenfeld, L., & Morville, P. (1998). *Information architecture for the World Wide Web.* Sebastopol, CA: O'Reilly.

Williams, R., & Tollett, J. (1997). *The non-designer's Web book.* Berkeley, CA: Peachpit Press.

Evaluating and selecting tools and software packages for creating Web learning:

Distance learning: Hotlinks. (1998, October). *Training,* pp. DL 1–22.

Khan, B., & Vega, R. (1997). Factors to consider when evaluating a Web-based instruction course: A survey. In B. Khan (Ed.), *Web-based instruction* (pp. 375–378). Englewood Cliffs, NJ: Educational Technology Publications.

Phillips, V. (1998, April). Selecting an on-line authoring system. *Training,* pp. 53–60.

Evaluating and selecting Web-based skills management software:

Auerbach, S. (1997, July/August). Mining for skills. *Inside Technology Training,* pp. 40–53.

Project management for Web-based training development:

Driscoll, M. (1998). *Web-based training.* San Francisco: Jossey-Bass/Pfeiffer, chapter 9.

COMMERCIAL TOOLS FOR CREATING WEB LEARNING ENVIRONMENTS

You need to be aware that most commercially available Web software tools focus on media management, not on instruction. Tools such as Microsoft FrontPage or Adobe PageMill give you templates for creating, coordinating, and displaying media such as text, video, audio, and graphics on the Web. Rarely do they include strategies or templates for making sure that those presentations are instructionally sound. However, presenting flashy graphics and complex simulations does not necessarily lead to learning. Hiltz's (1995) research, for example, found that learner achievement varied more by course organization, instructional design, and instructor effort than by the type or amount of media used. Years before the advent of the Web, Clark (1987, p. 154) concluded that "the best evidence is that media are mere vehicles that deliver instruction but do not influence achievement any more than the truck that delivers our groceries causes changes in our nutrition . . . only the content of the vehicle can directly influence nutrition and/or achievement."

Be careful in choosing commercial Web development tools; most of them focus on presentation of media, and do not embody any theories or models of teaching and learning. However, some tools are beginning to be developed that address the design of instruction for the Web. These tools are available from the Web sites listed here.

Web Sites That Offer Tools for Creating Web Learning Environments

Site	Tools
Avilar **http://www.avilar.co**	Webmentor: template-based tools for development, delivery, and training management of self-paced and asynchronous instructor-led learning, threaded discussions, e-mail, and bulletin boards
Asymetrix **http://www.asymetrix.com**	Toolbook II Instructor, Librarian, IconAuthor Net Edition, CMS Plus: Tools for development, delivery, remote administration, synchronous and collaborative learning, and training management
Blackboard **http://www.blackboard.net**	Web site and server management software for learning sites in large (enterprise) organizations
Centra **http://www.centra.com**	Symposium: Tools for managing instructor-led, collaborative synchronous learning environments
Computer Adaptive Technology **http://www.catinc.com**	Computer-based (including Web) test and survey development tools, item banking, test administration, registration
Connecticut River Interactive **http://www.ctriver.com**	Tools for Web-based synchronous instructor-led learning
CyberWISE (Saratoga Group) **http://www.cyberwise.com**	Tools for creating Web-based tests and training management systems; site also has a catalog of Information Technology courseware
Cytation Corporation **http://www.cytation.com**	Tools for Web training delivery and training management

Docent
http://www.docent.com

Outline-based development templates, automatic navigation creation from course outline, tools for delivering training from databases, training management software

Dynamic Diagrams, Inc.
http://www.dynamic diagrams.com

Tools and seminars for Web site architecture and mapping

Dyroweb
http://www.dyrowebic/wbt/ index.html

Guidelines and examples for creating Web-based training

Educational Object Economy
http://www.eoe.org

Free Java objects for education, plus research and articles

Flax
http://www.cms.dmu.ac.uk/ coursebook/flax

Tools for creating interactive Web pages and coursebooks

Formal Systems
http://www. formalsystems.com

Web-based test development tools

Intralearn
http://www.otm.com

Relational database, server-based tools for Web-based delivery and certification, training management, and asynchronous instructor-led learning

LearnerFirst
http://www.learner.first.com

Web-based knowledge management software

Live Training
http://www.livetraining.com

Tools for Web-based asynchronous delivery and training management

Lotus Learning Space (and DataBeam)
http://www.lotus.com/ learningspace

Tools to create Web-based, instructor-led synchronous and asynchronous learning environments and training management systems

Macromedia **http://www.macromedia.com**	Authorware Attain, Dreamweaver Attain, and Pathware: Visual authoring tools for development, delivery, content management, and training management using the Web and other delivery systems
Mentorware **http://www.mentorware.com**	Development, delivery, training management, and testing tools for various formats (including the Web)
Micromedium **http://www.micromedium.com**	Digital Trainer Professional: Development templates, "e-books," and tools for converting existing training materials to the Web
People Sciences **http://www.peoplesci.com**	Web-based skill assessment software
Phoenix **http://www.pathlore.com**	Database-based training development and management templates
Placeware **http://www.placeware.com**	Tools for managing synchronous Web learning classrooms and Web conferencing
Question Mark **http://www.questionmark.com**	Web-based test and survey development tools
Skillview Technologies **http://www.skillview.com**	Web-based skill assessment software
Softarc **http://www.softarc.com**	Software for Web-based collaboration
Stagecast **http://www.stagecast.com**	Tools for creating Web-based simulations
Street Technologies **http://www.streetinc.com**	Tools for Web-based learning delivery and training management

SyberWorks **http://www.syberworks.com**	Development and delivery tools, course catalogs, and Web hosting services
Synthesis Corporation, National Engineering Education Delivery System **http://www.needs.org**	‚Software, hardware, and support for the development and delivery of engineering-related courseware using the Web and other technologies
TeamScape Corporation **http://www.teamscape.com/ index.html**	Delivery and training management for large (enterprise) organizations
University of North Carolina, Chapel Hill **http://www.unc.edu/courses/ ssp/share**	Web learning development tools for nonprofit organizations and educational institutions
Vlearn **http://www.vlearn.com/ default.htm**	Tools for Web-based knowledge management, content delivery, and training management
WBT Systems **http://www.wbtsystems.com**	TopClass: Tools for creating (or converting and assembling from non-Web sources) asynchronous, collaborative learning environments and training management systems
Web Course in a Box (Virginia Commonwealth University) **http://madduck.mmd.vcu. edu/wcb/wcb.html**	HTML forms-based tools for developing and accessing Web learning
WebCT (University of British Columbia) **http://homebrew1.cs.ubc.ca/ webct**	Browser-based learning development and delivery tools
Wellengaged **http://www.wellengaged.com**	Client and server software to support on-line discussions and chat

DISTANCE LEARNING/ LOCAL LEARNING: LEARNING HAPPENS WHERE THE WORK IS

Libby Bishop, research scientist,
Institute for Research on Learning

Computer mediated learning—often called "distance learning"—represents, as yet, only a small share of total workplace training hours, but its growth is rapid and certain to accelerate. At the Institute for Research on Learning (IRL), we're trying to advance our understanding of how such distance learning is being done and how it might be done more effectively to ensure that technological developments don't end up recreating the kinds of ineffective training we often see in corporate classrooms.

Two of our seven Learning Principles (discussed in Chapter 4) are particularly important in making sense of how to create effective distance learning programs. First, "Knowing depends on engagement in practice." What is difficult to learn in the abstract is often more easily understood when it is a part of everyday life. At the very least, the motivation to learn is often greater when it is easy to see how learning might facilitate work (or play). Because of this, we often encourage corporations to move training out of centralized classrooms and into the work. Second, "Learning is fundamentally social." When we study learning in the world, we find that most often, it happens not by an individual, or even by an individual listening to and absorbing information presented by a teacher, but in engagements among people. In work settings, most of what people learn about their job, they learn through participation in communities of practice, communities of people who do the same (or closely related) work.

Computer mediated learning—especially web learning—offers an exciting opportunity to move training closer to work and therefore closer to facilitating learning in the context of work practice. One way of thinking about this is to recognize that distance learning is not, in fact, distant. Or at least, it is distant only from the training center, not from the workplace. We prefer to think of distance learning, when it truly integrates with actual work practice, as the true "local learning." At the same time, we believe it is essential to look carefully at what happens to the social aspects of learning when training shifts out of corporate training centers and into working offices. The local learning environment now includes the computer, Web access, colleagues in the office, and daily work activities, but may lack some of the social advantages of classroom learning.

Our work at IRL has paid special attention to the growing awareness of, and value placed upon, the social dimensions of on-line learning environments. New offerings now explicitly address concerns such as synchronous and asynchronous interaction, interactions with instructors and with other students, opportunities for collaborative tool use and text editing, and the formation of learning communities. *The exciting—but as yet unrealized opportunity—is to use the Web and related new technologies to integrate work and learning while supporting their fundamentally social character.*

In the next section, we present brief summaries of three cases, each one confronting a different mix of issues around work, learning, and technology. These cases reinforce many of the messages found in the preceding volume, and offer some additional ideas for consideration:

- Learning cannot rely on technology alone; the Web is one *element* in a learning strategy, it isn't a learning strategy in itself
- It's essential to support learning communities as well as learning technologies
- The Web does not eliminate the need for teachers, instructors, and facilitators; it does, however, mean there will be changes in how those people work
- A successful Web-enabled learning program requires a deep understanding of the existing learning environment, especially the social and tacit elements of learning in both formal and informal settings

- A deep understanding of existing work practices is vital to an effective integration of learning and work
- Knowledge of how people really work and learn is essential to making the most innovative use of new technologies to support both "distance" and "local" learning

The following cases demonstrate how IRL researchers apply research results in the co-design and implementation of learning environments customized to the work practices, technological infrastructure, and learning needs in three diverse organizations. The first case is a virtual sales training class that demonstrates the complexities of computer-mediated, work-based learning. The second is a networked community of seniors that reveals much about how to sustain learning communities at work. The third (under development) is a Web site intended to help teachers with their own professional development needs to learn mathematics.

Decentralized Advance Sales Training

Description of Context

Xerox depends in part on sales by a geographically dispersed workforce of indirect (outsourced) sales agents. As employees of small, independent businesses, costs of training were especially prohibitive in both direct travel costs and in lost revenue from time out of the field. Xerox felt that obstacles to training were contributing to reduced earnings, low job satisfaction, and unacceptably high turnover of this sales force.

Xerox wanted to make advanced training on both products and sales processes more accessible by lowering overall costs and increasing the availability of training. This was addressed by designing a virtual, electronic classroom that enabled employees to learn while working in their offices and without traveling to the centralized training facility. This virtual classroom emulated many of the features of the non-virtual, centralized course traditionally offered.

Description of Training

Participants accessed the greater part of the class materials using their computers to download training modules, some of which they completed off-line. Supplementing the training modules were substantial on-line activities including private chats, shared forums, and email exchange. To conclude each module, small groups of students collaborated on-line to solve an applied problem.

Well-designed Web-enabled learning engages diverse,
even inaccessible audiences

In the Xerox case, the sales agents had historically had an ambiguous relationship to the company. They worked closely with the product line, but did not participate in programs, such as orientation, provided for regular employees. This status had direct implications for their learning needs. For example, in addition to needing sales skills, these agents also needed to learn more about activities surrounding the sale itself: processing orders; handling customer complaints; and, in general, how to navigate and negotiate the company's processes and procedures. These activities required skills and knowledge that are often best developed through experience. For this reason, IRL recommended that the "classroom" provide enough opportunity for the sharing of these experiences through informal interactions.

One of the reasons most often cited for using Web-enabled learning is to reach a larger audience of learners than would be possible with more conventional delivery. Indeed, this seems to be an important advantage of computer mediated programs like the one Xerox developed. Moreover, if effective learning is, as IRL's and others' research suggests, less about transmitting knowledge than about bringing new members into a learning community, then the potential of Web-enabled learning is even greater.

This case suggests that Web-enabled technologies, if designed with in-depth knowledge of learning and work practices, can provide opportunities for learners to participate in the organization in new ways. The official purpose may be learning, but the effects can be broadened to include new forms of membership, a sense of belonging. As organizations interact with people in increasingly diverse relationships (temporary workers, independent contractors, outsourced suppliers) and as learning opportunities are seen as ever more valuable by many employees, there are opportunities to use technology enhanced learning environments to strengthen working relationships.

Flexible boundaries between work and learning call for hybrid solutions

One of the insights from this case is the complexity "integrating work and learning." Valorie Beer's book makes clear that to put learning on the Web for people whose work is not Web-based does not automatically result in embedding learning in the work. We agree.

For example, in the on-line training of sales reps, hands-on access to the equipment (both Xerox products and competitor's offerings) was not possible. This was obviously a major drawback; it is not possible to create a comprehensive learning environment for product sales that is exclusively Web-mediated.

However, the boundaries between what is real and what is virtual, and between what is work and what is learning, are not always clear or rigid. This case shows that even employees whose work practice had not been predominantly electronically mediated were able to make use of the advantages of an on-line classroom environment to enhance their learning. Moreover, some of these enhancements happened precisely because the technology allowed work and learning activities to co-mingle in time and space in ways that had not previously been possible. We offer some examples below.

Bringing Real Work Problems Into Learning Environments

One of the key advantages of Web-based learning is that people can remain at work, at least in the sense of not having to travel to a training center. For these reps, remaining in their workplaces afforded opportunities to integrate actual and urgent work issues into class exercises. For example, a rep facing a particularly challenging competitor would use the interactive features to solicit ideas from classmates on how to counter the competitor's product claims. The immediacy of the issues made for far more compelling applications than the typical hands-on classroom exercises.

Drawing on Multiple and Overlapping Communities of Practice

In another instance, a member of the class had a question about a specific feature of one of the company's products. She was able to draw from diverse communities: local ones such as office mates, service technicians, and even customers, and her virtual learning community of classmates, the instructor, and indirectly, their communities.

The intermingling of work and learning allows for greater
second-order learning by those not directly engaged in training

The flow of learning became more richly multidirectional. In several instances, sales representatives taking the class introduced recently learned content into their local work environment, thus involving local work colleagues in the learning process. Ideally, of course, learners bring content back from centralized classes too. However, computer mediation lends an immediacy and interactivity to the process; office mates could ask questions, which could in turn feed into the on-line class discussions.

Fine-grained learning is supported by the real-case
learning context of work

The everyday work activities of the virtual classroom students provided abundant learning opportunities in addition to those provided by the instructional content supplied through the course. This created the potential for a sort of natural case-based learning, or real-case learning, as participants often pulled issues from the work setting into their virtual discussions. Significantly, this allowed learners to absorb a level of detail generally missing in centralized classroom training. This level of detail allowed them to actually learn enough to be able to do the work at the end of the lesson, to truly be able to put the training into practice on the job.

The accumulation of these opportunities are part of what differentiate a training focus (just the content, ma'am) to a more organic, self sustaining, continuous learning environment.

SeniorNet: Learning in Networked Communities

This next case may seem a bit incongruous: we are not looking at employees engaged in workplace learning, but rather at seniors, many retired, using the Web for diverse forms of communication and interaction. However, there are underlying patterns to how learning happens—in communities of practice and often tacitly—and these patterns are visible whether learning is in the workplace or in a recreational chat room. Seniors' use of the Web uncovers the richness of an active community and illustrates the intertwining technical and social factors that make it valuable for its members. Understanding how to integrate and balance these technical and social factors is equally relevant to businesses that wish to use net communities in support of employee learning, and increasingly, for their suppliers and customers as well.

SeniorNet was founded twelve years ago to help seniors gain access to computing technology. SeniorNet supports robust networked communities on the Web and on America Online, and it sponsors over 100 volunteer-staffed Learning Centers. The site provides diverse forms of communication: asynchronous discussion roundtables, synchronous casual socializing in a café, various chat formats, and others.

Predictable Rhythms and Diverse Modes of Use

Network communities exhibit a complex mix of interaction styles and rhythms. This richness enables the depth of expression needed to nurture multi-layered relationships. And it is precisely the fact of multi-layered relationships, in contrast to one-dimensional interactions, that are a key component of community. Members keep track one another on SeniorNet. If I haven't heard from you for a week, and I know you are sporadic in posting, I wouldn't be worried. However, if I know you are on line everyday, I might phone you, or ask others if they know if you are OK.

Rhythms of use matter in designing work-based learning environments also. One of the benefits of Web-enabled training is that it can provide asynchronous learning opportunities, allowing people to learn at their own speed and at times most convenient for them. When instructors grapple with the nuances of blending asynchronous and synchronous activities, this issue of phasing the learning matters. The benefits of flexibility of asynchronous work are often tempered by the need for a group to stay together on at least some parts of the material in order for the synchronous interactions to be most meaningful.

Social facilitation needs as much (or more)
work as technical support

From its inception, SeniorNet has had an explicit purpose of fostering a sense of solidarity rather than developing an information clearinghouse. This is in rather sharp contrast to many learning/knowledge sites which adopt the attitude that if the content is "good enough," users will come. SeniorNet's alternative approach, which IRL supports, suggests that the causality is reversed: what constitutes a good site or useful content is determined by the needs and practices of community members.

SeniorNet puts a great deal of effort into social, as compared to technical, facilitation. This involves volunteer work to support new and existing members. For example, volunteers often identity newcomers to chats and threads and welcome them, ask icebreaker questions, and offer assistance. Although reliance on volunteers happened in part because of limited funds for paid staff, it has created a strong sense of personal investment among community members. As in any authentic community, membership has its privileges, but also its responsibilities.

This explicit attention to the social aspects of the community shows itself in a distinguishing characteristic of the site that members describe with appreciation as "civility." They often attribute civility to members being of a more mannerly generation. But politeness is also something that the paid staff tries to foster when moderating discussion groups. It is precisely this behavioral norm, supported by community members and paid staff, which attracts and retains members on SeniorNet. It is one reason they remain loyal to SeniorNet as the primary vehicle for Web access. There may be lessons here for designers struggling with how to retain Web-site visitors.

This case reinforces a central message of this book: as vital as it is to get the technology right, equal time and money will be needed to get the learning strategy and its community right.

Where, Exactly, Is the Local?

As we saw with the Xerox case above, a significant, if messy, finding seems to be that one of the most interesting aspects of the Web is not that it sharply differentiates virtual/distant from real/local, but rather that both poles get re-conceptualized and mixed in novel ways.

There is still a great deal of debate as to whether or not successful on-line communities require links between physical and virtual spaces. At least for SeniorNet, it is quite clear that on-line and real-world interactions are integrated in multiple ways. On-line interactions are reinforced by a significant number of face-to-face meetings, including local and national gatherings, groups arranging to travel together, visits to SeniorNet members who live in different cities, and informal meetings of co-located members. Phone calls supplement both Web-based and face-to-face interactions.

Once again, it is important to creatively mix the local and virtual. The relevant question is not: can Web-enabled environments duplicate face-to-face interactions? The subtle, but more interesting, questions are: What is each environment best suited to do? And in what new ways can we support learning and work communities using innovative hybrid environments?

Web-based Math Learning Communities for Middle-School Teachers

Our third case is a prospective one, currently being piloted at IRL. Web-based Math Learning Communities for Middle-School Teachers (WebMath) will be an on-line mathematics learning environment and community for middle-school teachers. The design and pilot have been informed by research by IRL and others on communities of practice and on building web-based communities.

WebMath is designed to help teachers develop their own mathematical practices, and deep conceptual understanding, as adult mathematicians. WebMath will consist of two math courses, facilitators' training, and community-building activities for teachers. WebMath courses will be hands-on and interactive, employing the web as an interactive technology resource. Teachers will learn mathematics by doing mathematics: by posing and solving problems, by making mathematical arguments, by modeling and proving, and by communicating their ideas and work with others.

Importance of Understanding Current Work Practice in Order to use Technology to Support Learning

WebMath will integrate with teachers' current professional development activities; it will not require teachers to join a whole new program with new ways of thinking and functioning. It would have been easier to design a stand-alone math learning program. However, in our previous work with teachers, we found that many—particularly those in urban districts deemed in need of fixing—are overwhelmed with reform programs and agendas. WebMath will work in tandem with existing programs that are helping teachers implement Standards-based math. The previous projects that IRL has done with middle-school math teachers and their students provided the depth of understanding necessary to inform the design of a suitable web-based learning environment.

Community and interactivity on-line are
what make the difference

To form a community of practice, people need to interact around common artifacts. They need to develop ways of talking together. They need to have roles, ways of participating, that are alternately central or peripheral to the community; and they need the ability to move from one role to another. WebMath is offered as a course, but the intent is also for the course participants to form a community of mathematics practitioners, with its own patterns of discourse. Teachers will be able to participate in diverse ways such as: virtual meetings and classrooms, a web-integrated whiteboard, chat rooms, interactive teacher web pages, and tools for asynchronous communication as well. Special attention will be devoted to constructing the social aspects of the community: personalized introductions, use of avatars (if desired), on-line social events, and norm setting (facilitators will explicitly model ways of participating).

Conclusion

The changing nature of technology and the global economy are taxing the conventional paradigm for learning, training, and work. This paradigm is based on a classroom-centric, instructor-led mode of formal training derived from our educational system for children and young, largely pre-employed adults. The ledger of difficulties is well known: the typical centralized classroom facility requires too much time away from the job, expensive travel by instructors and students, and costly maintenance of often underused facilities. The resulting training is often outdated by the time of its delivery. The web has introduced an important new technology that can—if used appropriately—address these problems.

An adequate alternative model must overcome the entrenched separation of learning and training from actual work. Specifically, a fundamental rethinking of corporate training should include:

- Radical restructuring of formal training, retaining those elements shown to be successful
- Recognition of, and support for, informal learning
- Deliberate leveraging of the strengths of both formal and informal methods and, most importantly, a leveraging of the symmetries between the two methods
- Use of the Web and other tools as elements to support a coherent and well-designed learning strategy

Sources

Many people at IRL contributed comments, encouragement, ideas, text, and more. In addition, significant material has been quoted either verbatim or with very minor editing for clarification from the following sources.

Cefkin, M., et al. (1997). *From Training to Learning: Preparing for Success in a Digital World.* IRL and Xerox Education and Learning Organization Final Report.

Institute for Research on Learning (forthcoming). *Managing the New Business Of Learning: Strategic Understanding You Can Put To Use on Monday Morning* (working title).

Ito, M., Adler, A., Linde, C., Mynatt, E. D., & O'Day, V. L. (forthcoming). *Broadening Access: SeniorNet and the Case for Diverse Network Communities.*

Knudsen, J., & Berg, R. (August 25, 1999). *Web-based Mathematics Learning Community for Middle-School Teachers.* Proposal to the National Science Foundation Directorate for Education and Human Resources.

Mynatt, E. D., Adler, A., Ito, M., Linde, C., & O'Day, V. L. (1999). *The Network Communities of SeniorNet.* Paper to be presented at European Computer Supported Cooperative Work Conference.

O'Day, V. L., Ito, M., Linde, C., Adler, A., & Mynatt, E. D. (1999). *Cemeteries, Oak Trees, and Black and White Cows: Learning to Participate on the Internet.* Paper to be presented at European Computer Supported Cooperative Learning Conference.

ANNOTATED WEB TEMPLATES

Be sure to see these on the book's Web site:

www.pfeiffer.com/beer.html

EXHIBIT 6.1. WEB CONTENT ORGANIZATION TEMPLATE.

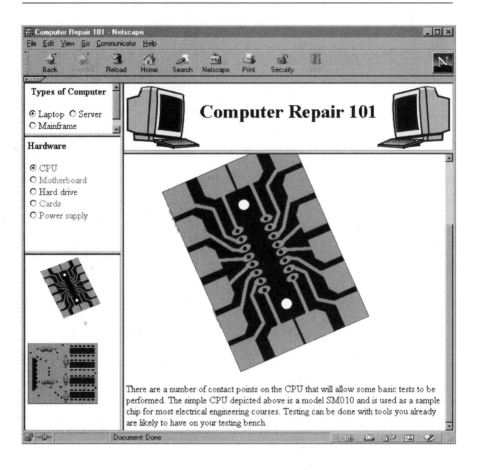

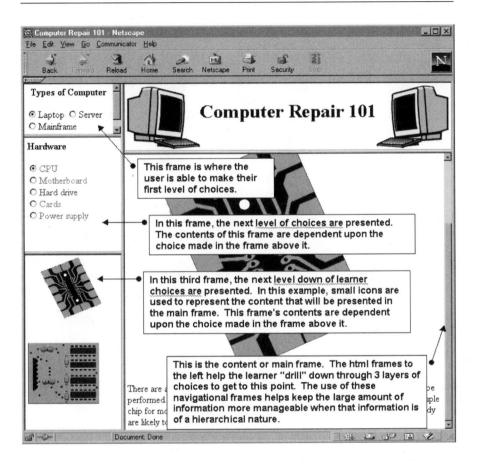

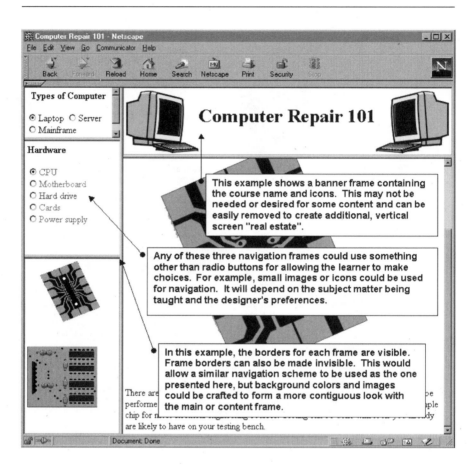

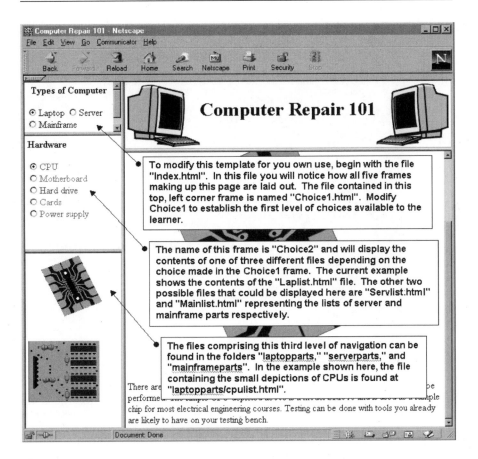

File Edit View Go Communicator Help

Back   Forward   Reload   Home   Search Netscape   Print   Security   Stop

Types of Computer

◉ Laptop ○ Server
○ Mainframe

Hardware

◉ CPU
○ Motherboard
○ Hard drive
○ Cards
○ Power supply

Computer Repair 101

To modify this template for you own use, begin with the file "Index.html". In this file you will notice how all five frames making up this page are laid out. The file contained in this top, left corner frame is named "Choice1.html". Modify Choice1 to establish the first level of choices available to the learner.

The name of this frame is "Choice2" and will display the contents of one of three different files depending on the choice made in the Choice1 frame. The current example shows the contents of the "Laplist.html" file. The other two possible files that could be displayed here are "Servlist.html" and "Mainlist.html" representing the lists of server and mainframe parts respectively.

The files comprising this third level of navigation can be found in the folders "laptopparts," "serverparts," and "mainframeparts". In the example shown here, the file containing the small depictions of CPUs is found at "laptopparts/cpulist.html".

There are performed. chip for most electrical engineering courses. Testing can be done with tools you already are likely to have on your testing bench.

Document: Done

EXHIBIT 7.1. WEB PRESENTATION
STRATEGY TEMPLATE.

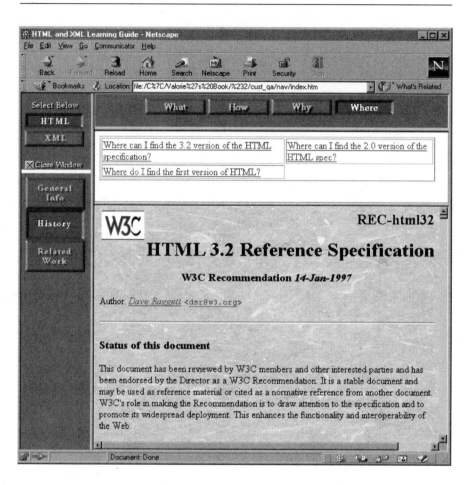

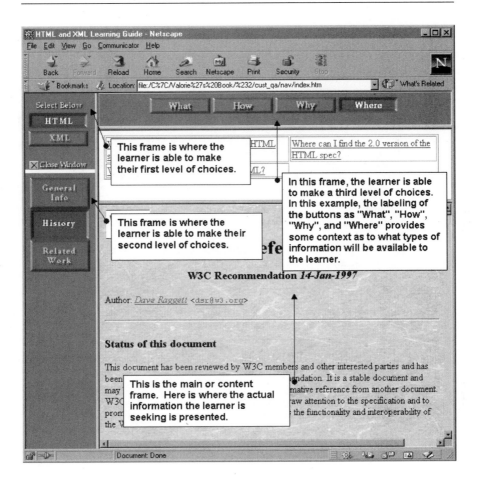

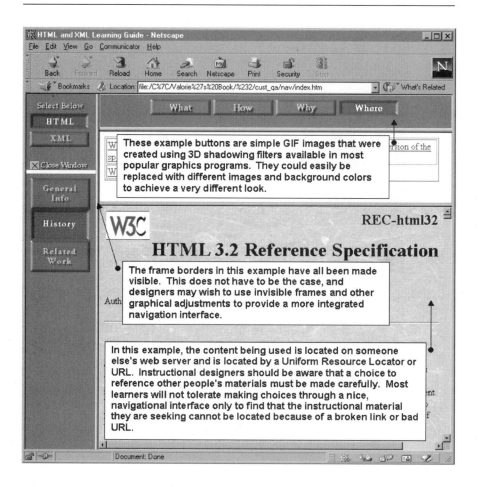

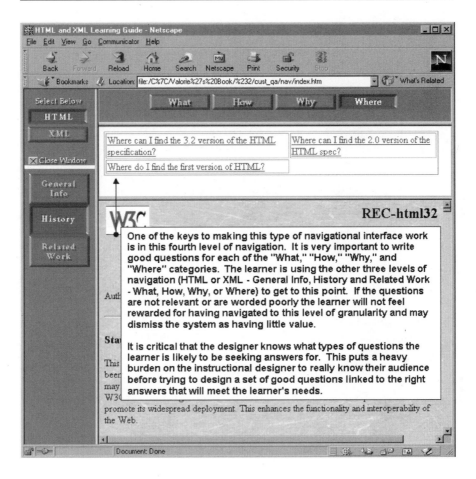

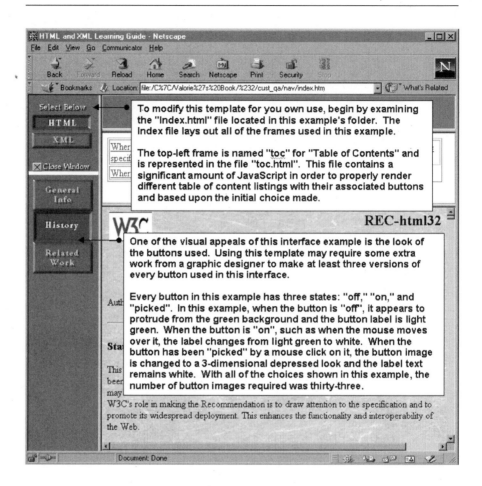

EXHIBIT 8.1. "LEARNING" AND "FINDING" ACTIVITIES TEMPLATE.

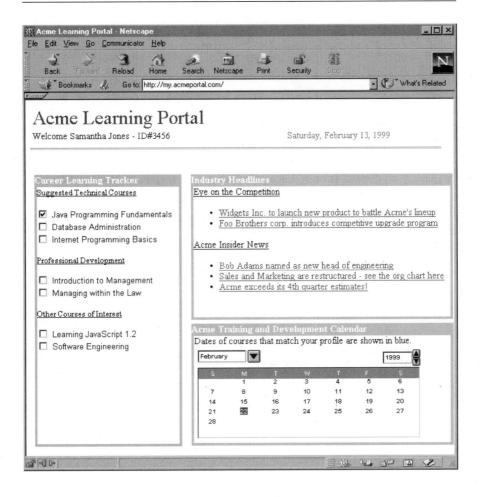

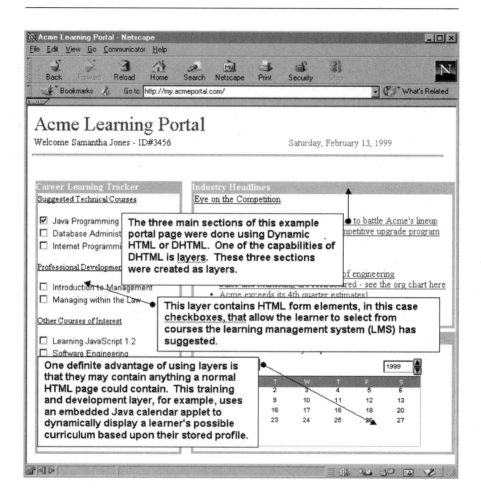

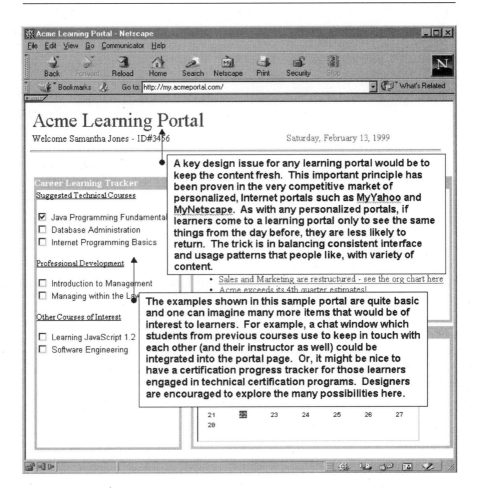

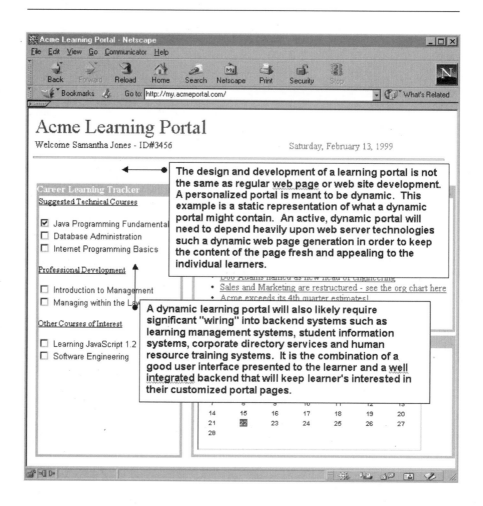

EXHIBIT 8.3. COLLABORATIVE WRITING AND EVALUATION ACTIVITY TEMPLATE.

Comments on Web Documents - Netscape

File Edit View Go Communicator Help

Back Forward Reload Home Search Netscape Print Security Stop

Extensible Markup Language (XML)

Many software developers see the Internet as the next great development opportunity. The rapid emergence of the Internet as a universal communications medium is due, in large part, to the quick establishment of a number of protocols and document formats. One of the most widely known and understood document formats is the HyperText Markup Language (HTML). After the initial euphoria of posting HTML documents on the web had passed, many developers looked to HTML as a means for Internet application development.

HTML has great capabilities for easily publishing web documents complete with formatting, custom fonts and multimedia elements. When it comes to web application development however, HTML shows some serious limitations. Bosak (1997) categorizes the three most severe limitations of HTML as:

- Extensibility. HTML does not allow users to specify their own tags or attributes in order to parameterize or otherwise semantically qualify their data. *I still don't understand how XML will*
- Structure. HTML does not support the specifi *achieve this goal. Maybe you could* it database schemas or object-oriented hierarchies. *provide more background as to how*
- Validation. HTML does not support the kind of *HTML tags ONLY cover page layout.* ng applications to check data for structural validity on importatic *You might also need to explain how communities will have to work out*

The World Wide Web Consortium (W3C) created a *accepted XML vocabularies in order to* enable the delivery of self-describing data structures of arbitra *form industry standards. - TA* quire such structures."(Bosak, 1997) The goal w as to remove t pment while at the same time, making the specification easy for develop produced the Extensible Markup Language (XML) specification which is a s ubset of the Standardized General Markup Language (SGML). SGML is also the parent language of HTML.

HTM *At this point, I think you need a graphic or some other* limitations inherent in respe *visual here. You might consider using a Venn diagram. - JC* L in three major

1
2
3   lications that need to

Submit Comment   Reset

The basic philosophy behind XML makes it perfect for marking up data in creating ways while still making that data

You are offline. Choose "Go Online..." to connect

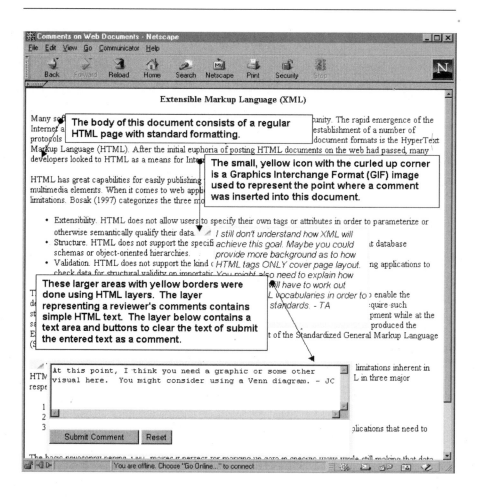

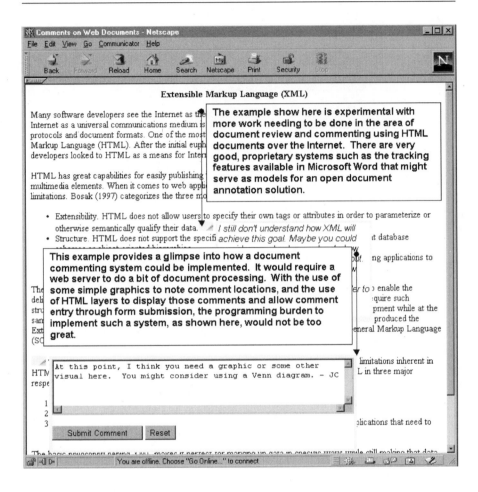

EXHIBIT 9.1. ASSESSMENT FEEDBACK
AND RESOURCES TEMPLATE.

Computer Repair Feeback Suggestions - Inbox - Netscape Folder   `_ □ ×`

File   Edit   View   Go   Message   Communicator   Help

| Get Msg | New Msg | Reply | Reply All | Forward | File | Next | Print | Delete | Stop | **N** |

Subject	Sender	Date
Online learning material change notification	Thor Anderson	8:17 PM
Computer Repair Feeback Suggestions	Thor Anderson	11:01 PM

Dear Samantha,

Our custom feedback engine has reviewed your scores for the "Computer Repair 101" series of courses you recently completed. We congratulate you on the successful completion of 14 out of the 16 courses in the series. There are, however, a few courses we think you may wish to revisit. Based upon a thorough review of your performance, we make the following suggestions:

Courses that should be taken over again:

Course Title - "CPU Troubleshooting and Replacement"
Reason: Your total score of 67 out of a possible 100 is not sufficient to pass this course.

Tips: You may not have spent as much time on this topic as is needed. Compared to the other courses where you averaged 1.65 hours per course, you only required 45 minutes for this course.

Course Title - "Diagnosing Video Card Problems"
Reason: Your total score of 28 out of a possible 38 is a passing grade, but is lower than your average score for the other courses you have completed.

Tips: Our records indicate a period of 76 days between when you took the Video Card Architecture course and the Diagnosing Video Card Problems course. You may wish to review the course "Video Card Architecture", which you performed well on, before taking the diagnosing course again. Many of the principles explained in the architecture course are relevant to the course on diagnosing problems.

You may re-enroll in any of these courses by selecting them.

Kind regards,

Online Learning Staff

Total messages: 203   Unread messages: 0

Computer Repair Feeback Suggestions - Inbox - Netscape Folder

File   Edit   View   Go   Message   Communicator   Help

| Get Msg | New Msg | Reply | Reply All | Forward | File | Next | Print | Delete | Stop |

Subject	Sender	Date
Online learning material change notification	Thor Anderson	8:17 PM
Computer Repair Feeback Suggestions	Thor Anderson	11:01 PM

Dear Samantha,

Our custom feedback engine has reviewed your scores for the "Computer Repair 101" series of courses
you recently completed. We congratulate you on the successful completion of 14 out of the 16 courses in
the series. There are, however, a few courses we think you may wish to revisit. Based upon a thorough
review of your performance, we make the

**This is an example email message that could
be sent to individual learners from a learning
management system.**

Courses that should be taken over again:

Course Title - "CPU Troubleshooting and Replacement"
Reason: Your total score of 67 out of a possible 100 is not sufficient to pass this course.

Tips: You may not have spent as much time on this topic as is needed. Compared to the other courses
where you averaged 1.65 hours per course, you only required 45 minutes for this course.

Course Title - "Diagnosing Video Card Problems"
Reason: Your total score of 28 out of a possible 38 is a passing grade, but is lower than your average
score for the other courses you have completed.

Tips: Our records indicate a p
course and the Diagnosing Vic
Card Architecture", which you
the principles explained in the

**Notice the use of embedded URLs that point to the
location of online courses the learning management
system is aware of. Most email readers handle URLs
embedded in the message quite well and email
notification is a handy manner for a training system to
communicate with learners.**

You may re-enroll in any of th

Kind regards,

Online Learning Staff

Total messages: 203   Unread messages: 0

Computer Repair Feeback Suggestions - Inbox - Netscape Folder

File   Edit   View   Go   Message   Communicator   Help

Get Msg   New Msg   Reply   Reply All   Forward   File   Next   Print   Delete   Stop

Subject	Sender	Date
Online learning material change notification	Thor Anderson	8:17 PM
Computer Repair Feeback Suggestions	Thor Anderson	11:01 PM

Dear Samantha,

Our custom feedback engine has reviewed your scores for the "Computer Repair 101" series of courses you recently completed. We congratulate you on the successful completion of 14 out of the 16 courses in the series. There are, ho...

review of your performa...

Courses that should be...

Course Title - "CPU Tr...
Reason: Your total scor...

> This example illustrates how a learning management system might take advantage of email to communicate with learners.   A learning management system does not have to be overly intelligent to provide useful information about how the learner performed in previous courses. Simple measures such as time spent for a given topic can help the management system provide learner guidance.

Tips: You may not have spent as much time on this topic as is needed. Compared to the other courses where you averaged 1.65 hours per course, you only required 45 minutes for this course.

Course Title - "Diagnosing Video Card Problems"
Reason: Your total score of 28 out of a possible 38 is a passing grade, but is lower than your average score for the other courses you have completed.

Tips: Our records indicate a period of 76 days between when you took the Video Card Architecture course and the Diagnosing Video Card Problems course. You may wish to review the course "Video Card Architecture", which you performed well on, before taking the diagnosing course again. Many of the principles explained in the architecture course are relevant to the course on diagnosing problems.

You may...

Kind reg...

Online L...

> Such tips as the one presented here demonstrate a more adaptive learning system than most people have had experience with. Even though the data is rather primitive, learners may be more motivated to take courses when some notice has been taken of their time spent in a topic and how well they performed on a given topic.

Total messages: 203   Unread messages: 0

EXHIBIT 9.2. SELF-ASSESSMENT TEMPLATE.

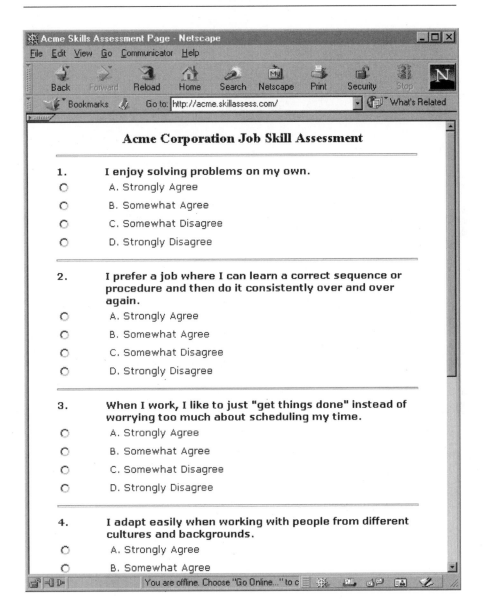

Acme Skills Assessment Page - Netscape

File   Edit   View   Go   Communicator   Help

Back   Forward   Reload   Home   Search   Netscape   Print   Security   Stop   N

Bookmarks   Go to: http://acme.skillassess.com/   What's Related

Acme Corporation Job Skill Assessment

1.   I enj

  ○   A. St

  ○   B. So

  ○   C. So

  ○   D. St

> These radio buttons are simple HTML Form elements. They are very easy to embed in HTML pages and there are many Common Gateway Interface (CGI) scripts available for processing form data.

2.   I prefer a job where I can learn a correct sequence or procedure and then do it consistently over and over again.

  ○   A. Strongly Agree

  ○   B. Somewhat Agree

  ○   C. So

  ○   D. St

> One can imagine many ways for a training developer to make use of HTML forms. An obvious, but often unused application would be for pre and post-test skill assessment. Another common use would be for course feedback data.

3.   When
worry

  ○   A. Strongly Agree

  ○   B. Somewhat Agree

  ○   C. Somewhat Disagree

  ○   D. Strongly Disagree

4.   I adapt easily when working with people from different cultures and backgrounds.

  ○   A. Strongly Agree

  ○   B. Somewhat Agree

You are offline. Choose "Go Online..." to c

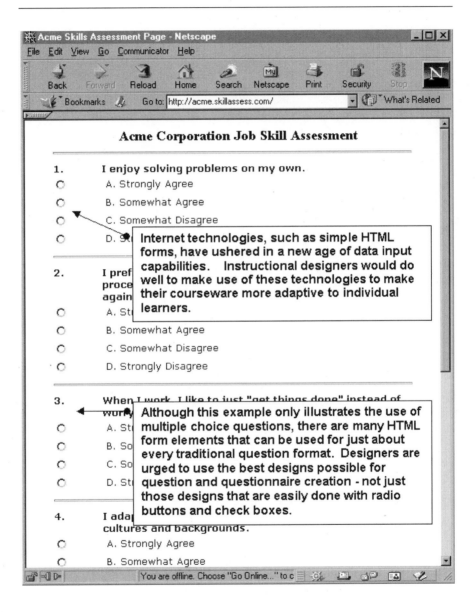

EXHIBIT 9.3. SELF-ASSESSMENT FEEDBACK
AND RESOURCES TEMPLATE.

Skills Assessment Results Page - Netscape

File Edit View Go Communicator Help

Back Forward Reload Home Search Netscape Print Security Stop

Acme Skills Assessment results for: Samantha Jones

Date of assessment: 2/22/99

SCORE:

Your overall score is 36 out of 50. This suggests that you have an aptitude for managing people, but should consider taking some courses to sharpen your managerial skills. Category results are listed below. Course suggestions are provided at the bottom of this document.

Basic Management Skills	4 of 4
Time Management	4 of 6
Managing Groups and Teams	6 of 10
Dealing with Budgets	7 of 8
Motivating Employees	5 of 6
Task Management	5 of 5
Advanced Managing Skills	5 of 8

Total Score 36/50

Your scores show a solid knowledge of entry level Management. Picking up some specific training on managing groups and teams will help you. You will also benefit from a review of advanced Managing skills. Combined with what you already know, these additional courses will give you the tools to advance toward the "Intermediate" manager level within Acme.

Suggested Courses: (click on course name to enroll)

Team Management - offered by ManagePro Inc.

Advanced Corporate Management - offered by ManagePro Inc.

Document: Done

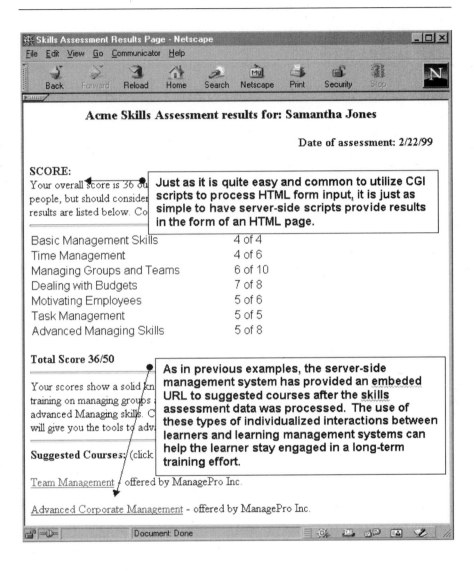

Acme Skills Assessment results for: Samantha Jones

Date of assessment: 2/22/99

SCORE:

Your overall score is 36 ou[t] ... people, but should consider ... results are listed below. Co...

> Just as it is quite easy and common to utilize CGI scripts to process HTML form input, it is just as simple to have server-side scripts provide results in the form of an HTML page.

Basic Management Skills	4 of 4
Time Management	4 of 6
Managing Groups and Teams	6 of 10
Dealing with Budgets	7 of 8
Motivating Employees	5 of 6
Task Management	5 of 5
Advanced Managing Skills	5 of 8

Total Score 36/50

Your scores show a solid kn[owledge] ... training on managing group[s] ... advanced Managing skill[s]. C... will give you the tools t[o] adv...

> As in previous examples, the server-side management system has provided an embeded URL to suggested courses after the skills assessment data was processed. The use of these types of individualized interactions between learners and learning management systems can help the learner stay engaged in a long-term training effort.

Suggested Courses: (click ...

Team Management [—] offered by ManagePro Inc.

Advanced Corporate Management - offered by ManagePro Inc.

Skills Assessment Results Page - Netscape

File Edit View Go Communicator Help

Back Forward Reload Home Search Netscape Print Security Stop

Acme Skills Assessment results for: Samantha Jones

Date of assessment: 2/22/99

SCORE:
Your overall score is 36 out of 50. This suggests that you have an aptitude for managing people, but should consider taking some courses to sharpen your managerial skills. Category results are listed below. Course suggestions are provided at the bottom of this document.

Basic Management S
Time Management
Managing Groups and
Dealing with Budgets
Motivating Employees
Task Management
Advanced Managing Skills   5 of 8

> Internet technologies can allow more two-way interaction between the learner and the learning management system. Progress reports, such as the one shown here, are only one of many methods for enhancing the communication between learners and learning system software.

Total Score 36/50

Your scores show a solid kn
training on managing groups
advanced Managing skills. C
will give you the tools to adv

> The use of URLs in this progress report make it potentially more active than just a passive reporting of skills assessment data. Suggested courses as URLs invite the learner to do something by following the link provided. This is another design principle that can help foster more interaction between learners and learning systems.

Suggested Courses: (click

Team Management offered by ManagePro Inc.

Advanced Corporate Management - offered by ManagePro Inc.

Document: Done

EXHIBIT 9.4. LEARNING RESOURCE
UPDATE TEMPLATE.

Online learning material change notification - Inbox - Netscape Folder

File Edit View Go Message Communicator Help

Get Msg New Msg Reply Reply All Forward File Next Print Delete Stop

Inbox   Total messages: 203   Unread messages: 1

Subject	Sender	Date
Online learning material change notification	Thor Anderson	8:17 PM
Computer Repair Feeback Suggestions	**Thor Anderson**	**8:17 PM**

Dear Samantha,

Our course content search engine has found new, targeted course materials that will likely be of interest to you. By matching your online learning profile with our newest course offerings, we suggest you take a look at the following:

New Topic Suggestions:

Course Title = "Advanced Java: Virtual Machines and Threads"
Suggested Topic#1 = "Garbage Collection in the Virtual Machine"
Suggested Topic#2 = "Writing Threads for Multiprocessor machines"

Also, the content search engine has found that a new topic was recently added to a previous course you have taken.

Previous Course Title = "Accessing Databases using Java"
New Suggested Topic#1 = "Understanding JSQL"

You may enroll in any of these topics by selecting them. We hope you find this service useful.

Kind regards,

Online Learning Staff

Online learning material change notification - Inbox - Netscape Folder

File Edit View Go Message Communicator Help

Get Msg   New Msg   Reply   Reply All   Forward   File   Next   Print   Delete   Stop

Inbox   Total messages: 203   Unread messages: 1

	Subject		Sender	Date
	Online learning material change notification		Thor Anderson	8:17 PM
	Computer Repair Feeback Suggestions		**Thor Anderson**	**8:17 PM**

Dear Samantha,

Our course content s   will likely be of interest to
you. By matching yo   we suggest you take a look
at the following:

New Topic Suggesti

Course Title = "Advanced Java: Virtual Machines and Threads
Suggested Topic#1 = "Garbage Collection in the Virtual Machine"
Suggested Topic#2 = "Writing Threads for Multiprocessor machines"

Also, the content search engine has found that a new topic was recently added to a previous course you
have taken.

Previous Course Title = "Accessing Data
New Suggested Topic#1 = "Understandin

You may enroll in any of these topics by

Kind regards,

Online Learning Staff

> **Email can be a great mechanism for reaching learners in an asynchronous manner. It is also very flexible in that most email programs read HTML-based email messages. This allows links, such as the ones shown below, to be embedded in the body of the message.**

> **Another important feature of email is the ability for learning management systems and other software tools to automatically generate and send email. When done properly, such automation can greatly reduce the communication burdens of a training staff.**

Online learning material change notification - Inbox - Netscape Folder

File Edit View Go Message Communicator Help

Get Msg   New Msg   Reply   Reply All   Forward   File   Next   Print   Delete   Stop

Inbox   Total messages: 203   Unread messages: 1

Subject	Sender	Date
Online learning material change notification	Thor Anderson	8:17 PM
Computer Repair Feeback Suggestions	**Thor Anderson**	**8:17 PM**

Dear Samantha,

Our course content search engine has found new, targeted course materials that will likely be of interest to you. By matching your online learning profile with our newest course offerings, we suggest you take a look at the following:

As more instructional resources are cataloged and made available on the Internet, it will be possible for search engines to locate content that matches the learner's particular learning profile. There are current efforts underway in the online learning community to define standard mechanisms for identifying content and for specifying learning profile information.

New Topic Suggestions:

Course Title = "Advanced Java:
Suggested Topic#1 = "Garbage
Suggested Topic#2 = "Writing Tl

Also, the content search engine has found that a new topic was recently added to a previous course you have taken.

Previous Course Title = "Accessing Databases using Java"
New Suggested Topic#1 = "Understanding JSQL"

You may enroll in any of these topics by selecting them. We hope you find this service useful.

Kind regards,

Online Learning Staff

EXHIBIT 9.5. WEB LEARNING
FEEDBACK TEMPLATE.

Feedback Form - Netscape

File   Edit   View   Go   Communicator   Help

Back   Forward   Reload   Home   Search   Netscape   Print   Security   Stop

Bookmarks   Go to: http://Acme.comprepair.com/feedback   What's Related

Computer Repair 101 Feedback Form

Thank you for checking out our latest course in the Computer Repair series. We would appreciate you taking a few moments to give us some feedback.

1. Which titles best describe your current job? (check all that apply)
- ☐ Repair Technician
- ☐ Hardware Specialist
- ☐ Consultant
- ☐ Programmer
- ☐ Other (Please specify) [   ]

2. Have you ever taken a technical course using the Internet before?
○ Yes   ○ No   ○ I've taken other courses - not technical ones

3. How familiar are you with the Computer Repair series of online courses?
○ Very   ○ Somewhat   ○ Just a little   ○ Not at all

4. How would you rate your overall experience with the Computer Repair 101 course?
○ Excellent   ○ Very Good   ○ Good   ○ Poor   ○ Very Bad

5. Were you able to successfully launch and complete the course?
○ Yes   ○ No   ○ Partially (Please explain your response below)

[   ]

6. What kinds of other Computer Repair courses would you like to see in the future?

You are offline. Choose "Go Online..." to connect

This example makes use of many HTML form elements to solicit course feedback from the learner. Internet technologies, such as forms processing, can be leveraged to provide much more automatic data input and processing than many traditional training departments were able to do in the past.

Feedback Form - Netscape

File Edit View Go Communicator Help

Back   Forward   Reload   Home   Search   Netscape   Print   Security   Stop

Bookmarks   Go to: http://Acme.comprepair.com/feedback   What's Related

Computer Repair 101 Feedback Form

Thank you for checking out our latest course in the Computer Repair series. We would appreciate you taking a few moments to give us some feedback.

1. Which titles best describe your current job? (check all that apply)
- ☐ Repair Technician
- ☐ Hardware Specialist
- ☐ Consultant
- ☐ Programmer
- ☐ Other (Please specify)

2. Have you ever taken a technical course u
○ Yes ○ No ○ I've taken other courses - not

3. How familiar are you with the Computer R
○ Very ○ Somewhat ○ Just a little ○ Not

4. How would you rate your overall experien
○ Excellent ○ Very Good ○ Good ○ Poor

5. Were you able to successfully launch and
○ Yes ○ No ○ Partially (Please explain you

> This example is not intended to serve as an example of proper feedback form design. As a matter of fact, this example is based upon traditional feedback form design, which is rather passive and static. One can imagine using contextual questions that cause additional questions to appear based upon the learner having chosen them.
>
> For example, once a radio button is selected a JavaScript function could cause a window to appear that prompts the learner for additional input. This rather simple use of Internet technology would produce a much more adaptive and interactive feedback form than most learners are accustomed to.

6. What kinds of other Computer Repair courses would you like to see in the future?

You are offline. Choose "Go Online..." to connect

EXHIBIT 10.2. INSTRUCTOR WEB SITE TEMPLATE.

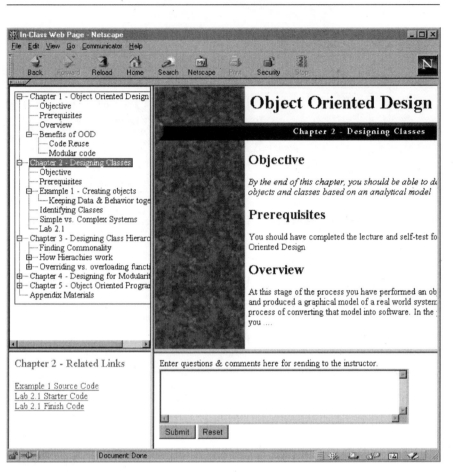

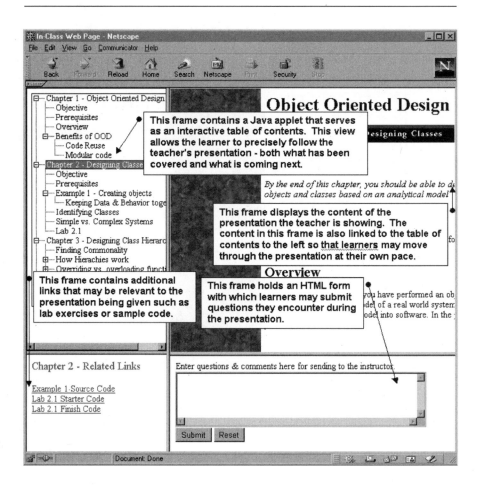

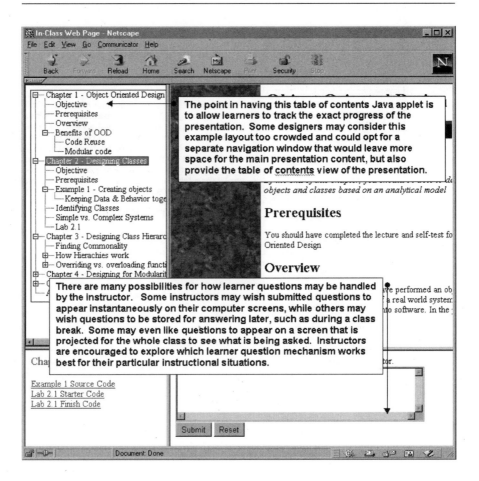

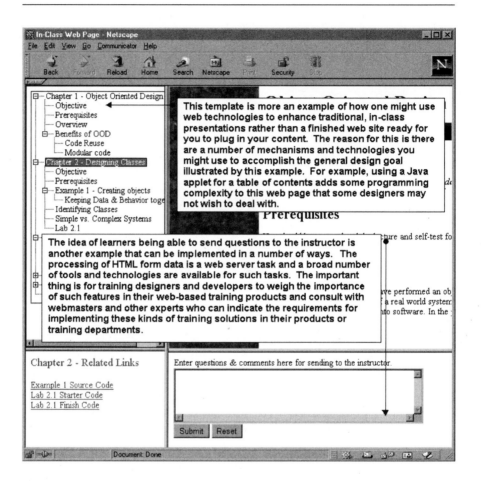

APPENDIX D

REFERENCES

Ambrosio, J. (1998, November 25). Job training moves online, but not without bumps. *Computerworld Online News.*

Barlow, J. (1998, January). A confederacy of apprentices. *Training,* pp. 44–50.

Bonk, C. J., & Reynolds, T. H. (1997). Learner-centered Web instruction for higher-order thinking, teamwork, and apprenticeship. In B. Khan (Ed.), *Web-based instruction* (pp. 167–178). Englewood Cliffs, NJ: Educational Technology Publications.

Bassi, L., Cheney, S., & Van Buren, M. (1997, November). Training industry trends. *Training,* pp. 46–59.

Butler, B. S. (1997). Using the World Wide Web to support classroom-based education: Conclusions from a multiple-case study. In B. Khan (Ed.), *Web-based instruction* (pp. 417–423). Englewood Cliffs, NJ: Educational Technology Publications.

Clark, R. E. (1987). The role of media in the evaluation of training. In L. S. May, C. A. Moore, & S. J. Zammit (Eds.), *Evaluating Business and Industry Training* (pp. 153–167). Boston: Kluwer Academic Publishers.

Driscoll, M. (1998). *Web-based training: Using technology to design adult learning experiences.* San Francisco: Jossey-Bass/Pfeiffer.

Duchastel, P. (1997). A motivational framework for Web-based instruction. In B. Khan (Ed.), *Web-based instruction* (pp. 179–184). Englewood Cliffs, NJ: Educational Technology Publications.

Einstein, D. (1998, October 30). Worldwide database of schools. *San Francisco Chronicle,* pp. B1–B2.

Esque, T. J. (1998, March). The Web: Of 'medium' importance to training? *Performance Improvement, 37*(3), 45–47.

Gillani, B. B., & Relan, A. (1997). Incorporating interactivity and multimedia into Web-based instruction. In B. Khan (Ed.), *Web-based instruction* (pp. 231–237). Englewood Cliffs, NJ: Educational Technology Publications.

Gordon, J. (1997, July). Info nuggets: The bite-sized future of corporate training? *Training,* pp. 26–33.

Hall, B. (1997). *Web-based training: Market trends, risks, and opportunities.* Sunnyvale, CA: Multimedia & Internet Training Newsletter.

Hanley, G. L., Schneebeck, C., & Zweier, L. (1998). *Implementing a scalable and sustainable model for instructional software development.* Long Beach: California State University, http://www.cdl.edu/html/syllabus98.html.

Harmon, A. (1998, August 30). Internet use linked to decline in well-being. *San Francisco Chronicle,* pp. A1, A7.

Henschel, P. (1996). Embedded in community. *Wingspread Journal,* p. 12.

Hiltz, S. R. (1995, March). Teaching in a virtual classroom. Paper presented at the International Conference on Computer Assisted Instruction, Hsinchu, Taiwan.

Horton, W. (1997, March). New media: An assay for managers. *Performance Improvement, 36*(3), 18–22.

Hudspeth, D. (1997). Testing learner outcomes in Web-based instruction. In B. Khan (Ed.), *Web-based instruction* (pp. 353–356). Englewood Cliffs, NJ: Educational Technology Publications.

Jonassen, D. H., Grabinger, R. S., & Harris, N. D. C. (1997). Analyzing and selecting instructional strategies and tactics. *Performance Improvement Quarterly, 10*(1), 34–54.

Lippincott, J. (1998, September). Interview with Chris Newell, executive director, Lotus Institute. *Performance Improvement, 37*(7), 37–39.

Management in cyberspace. (1998, August 15). *Economist,* p. 68.

Manasco, B. (1996, October). Enterprise-wide learning: Corporate knowledge networks and the new learning imperative. Knowledge Inc., http://www.Webcom.com/quantera/enterprise.html.

McKegney, M. (1997, September 8). Training via Nets starts to heat up. *Web Week,* pp. 17–18.

Merrill, M. D. (1994). The descriptive component display theory. In M. D. Merrill and D. G. Twitchell (Eds.), *Instructional design theory* (pp. 111–157). Englewood Cliffs, NJ: Educational Technology Publications.

Merrill, M. D. (1997, April). Presentation at the Annual Conference of the International Society for Performance Improvement, Anaheim, California.

Merrill, M. D. (1998, June). Wake up (and reclaim instructional design). *Training,* pp. 36–42.

Miller, B. (1998, May/June). Document management: An interview with Jim Boyle and Larry Bielawski. *Performance Improvement, 37*(5), 32–35.

Norman, D. A. (1988). *The psychology of everyday things.* New York: Basic Books.

Paul, L. G. (1997, April 29). It's payback time, folks. *PC Week Online,* http://www.zdnet.com/pcweek.

Ravitz, J. (1997). Evaluating learning networks: A special challenge for Web-based instruction. In B. Khan (Ed.), *Web-based instruction* (pp. 361–368). Englewood Cliffs, NJ: Educational Technology Publications.

Reigeluth, C. M., Merrill, M. D., Wilson, B. G., & Spiller, R. T. (1994). The elaboration theory of instruction: A model for sequencing and synthesizing instruction. In M. D. Merrill and D. G. Twitchell (Eds.), *Instructional design theory* (pp. 79–91). Englewood Cliffs, NJ: Educational Technology Publications.

Report: Sales of online curriculum to K–12 market will hit $10 million in '97. (1997, November 19). *Electronic Education Report, 4*(22), 5–7.

Romiszowski, A. (1997). Web-based distance learning and teaching: Revolutionary invention or reaction to necessity? In B. Khan (Ed.), *Web-based instruction* (pp. 25–37). Englewood Cliffs, NJ: Educational Technology Publications.

Rose, R. (1998, January). Detour on the I-way. *Training,* pp. 70–78.

Rosenfeld, L., & Morville, P. (1998). *Information architecture for the World Wide Web.* Sebastopol, CA: O'Reilly.

Rossett, A., Keenan, C., & Adgate, G. (1997, September). 'Aztechnology turns:' A World Wide Web soap opera about change in the profession. *Performance Improvement, 36*(8), 20–25.

Semilof, M. (1997, February 13). Inchworm, inchworm, measuring the Internet. *Techwire,* http://www.techweb.com.

Seven principles of learning. (1990). Menlo Park, CA: Institute for Research on Learning.

Sherry, L., & Wilson, B. (1997). Transformative communication as a stimulus to Web innovations. In B. Khan (Ed.), *Web-based instruction* (pp. 67–73). Englewood Cliffs, NJ: Educational Technology Publications.

Shotsberger, P. G. (1997). Emerging roles for instructors and learners in the Web-based instruction classroom. In B. Khan (Ed.), *Web-based instruction* (pp. 101–106). Englewood Cliffs, NJ: Educational Technology Publications.

Snyder, W. M. (1997). *Communities of practice: Combining organization learning and strategy insights to create a bridge to the twenty-first century.* Cambridge, MA: Social Capital Group.

Stamps, D. (1997, February). Communities of practice: Learning is social, training is irrelevant? *Training,* pp. 34–41.

Wenger, E. (1996, July/August). Communities of practice: The social fabric of a learning organization. *Healthcare Forum Journal, 39*(4), 20–26.

Why paper won't go away. (1998, April). *Training,* pp. 37–44.

Williams, V., & Peters, K. (1997). Faculty incentives for the preparation of Web-based instruction. In B. Khan (Ed.), *Web-based instruction* (pp. 107–110). Englewood Cliffs, NJ: Educational Technology Publications.

Young, J. R. (1997). Rethinking the role of the professor in an age of high-tech tools. *Chronicle of Higher Education,* http://chronicle.com/colloquy/97/unbundle/background.htm.

APPENDIX E

ADDITIONAL RESOURCES FOR READING AND BROWSING

Instructional Design and Evaluation

Beer, V., & Bloomer, A. C. (1986). Levels of evaluation. *Educational Evaluation and Policy Analysis, 8*(4), 335–346.

Goldstein, I. L. (1992). *Training in organizations: Needs assessment, development, and evaluation.* Pacific Grove, CA: Brooks/Cole.

Hall, B., & Sprenger, P. (1997, July). Team training. *Internet World,* pp. 58–60.

Khan, B., & Vega, R. (1997). Factors to consider when evaluating a Web-based instruction course: A survey. In B. Khan (Ed.), *Web-based instruction* (pp. 375–378). Englewood Cliffs, NJ: Educational Technology Publications.

Merrill, M. D., & Twitchell, D. G. (Eds.). (1994). *Instructional design theory.* Englewood Cliffs, NJ: Educational Technology Publications.

Rossett, A. (1987). *Training needs assessment.* Englewood Cliffs, NJ: Educational Technology Publications.

Zemke, R., & Kramlinger, T. (1982). *Figuring things out.* Reading, MA: Addison-Wesley.

Learning Theory

Brown, J. S., Collins, A., & Duguid, P. (1989, January-February). Situated cognition and the culture of learning. *Educational Researcher,* pp. 32–42.

Cognitive Arts (formerly the Institute for Learning Sciences)—http://www.lscorp.com.

Cornell, R., & Martin, B. L. (1997). The role of motivation in Web-based instruction. In B. Khan (Ed.), *Web-based instruction* (pp. 93–100). Englewood Cliffs, NJ: Educational Technology Publications.

Duchastel, P. (1997). A motivational framework for Web-based instruction. In B. Khan (Ed.), *Web-based instruction* (pp. 179–184). Englewood Cliffs, NJ: Educational Technology Publications.

Institute for Research on Learning—http://www.irl.org.

Web Learning Market Analysis

Hall, B. (1997). *Web-based training: Market trends, risks, and opportunities.* Sunnyvale, CA: Multimedia & Internet Training Newsletter.

Hall, B. (1997). *Web-based training cookbook.* New York: Wiley.

McKegney, M. (1997, September 8). Training via Nets starts to heat up. Web Week, pp. 17–18.

Web Site Design

Berst, J. (1998, October 8). Don't make this Web site mistake. ZDNet Anchor Desk—for the general site: http://www.zdnet.com/anchordesk; for this specific article: http://www.zdnet.com/anchordesk/story_index_19981008.html.

Bielawski, L., & Boyle, J. (1996) *Electronic document management systems.* Princeton, NJ: Prentice Hall.

Building a better interface—complete list of tips and picks

C|Net Builder.com—http://www.builder.com.

Dynamic Diagrams, Inc.—http://www.dynamicdiagrams.com.

Tools and seminars for Web site architecture and mapping

Dyroweb—http://www.dyrowebic/wbt/index.html.

Guidelines and examples for creating Web-based training

Flanders, V., & Willis, M. (1996). *Web pages that suck.* San Francisco: Sybex.

Jones, M. G., & Farquhar, J. D. (1997). User interface design for Web-based instruction. In B. Khan (Ed.), *Web-based instruction* (pp. 239–244). Englewood Cliffs, NJ: Educational Technology Publications.

Nielsen, J. (1996, May). Top ten mistakes in Web design. Sun Microsystems Alert Box, http://www.sun.com/960416/columns/alertbox/index.html; see also Jakob Nielsen's user interface design site—http://www.useit.com/alertbox.

Rosenfeld, L., & Morville, P. (1998). *Information architecture for the World Wide Web.* Sebastopol, CA: O'Reilly.

Williams, R., & Tollett, J. (1997). *The non-designer's Web book.* Berkeley, CA: Peachpit Press.

GLOSSARY

applet
Small Java program that can be embedded in an HTML page.

asynchronous
Events that take place independently in time or with a time delay.

bandwidth
The amount of network capacity available to carry files, e-mail, and other materials from one place on a network to another.

browser
An application that enables users to access various kinds of Internet and intranet resources such as HTML files, video, audio, and images.

electronic whiteboard
An application that enables two or more users to share a Web-based "chalk-board" device.

HTML (See Hypertext Markup Language)

HTPP (See Hypertext Transfer Protocol)

Note: Adapted from Driscoll, M. (1998). *Web-based training: Using technology to design adult learning experiences.* San Francisco: Jossey-Bass/Pfeiffer.)

hypertext

Text or other medium that can be chosen by a learner and that causes another document or medium to be retrieved and displayed.

Hypertext Markup Language (HTML)

A coding language used to mark up documents for use on the Web. Some HTML codes define the basic appearance—size, type of font, layout, and so on—of a document, regardless of the type of equipment and software used to present that document to the reader. Other HTML codes allow text or graphics to be linked to resources (images, sound, video, and text) elsewhere on the same page or on another page on the Internet.

Hypertext Transfer Protocol (HTTP)

Rules and protocols for the Web that enable communication between servers and browsers.

instructional strategy

An overview of how information will be presented and how learners and instructors will interact in a training program.

intranet

An internal network that can stand alone or be connected to the Internet. In the latter case, incoming access from the Internet may be restricted in an effort to protect the sponsoring organization's security.

Java

A network-oriented programming language invented by Sun Microsystems. Java was specifically designed for writing programs that can be downloaded from the Internet to the desktop and immediately run.

multimedia

The use of two or more of the following elements in a computer-based training program: text, images, video, audio, and animation.

netiquette

The etiquette or rules of behavior for the Internet.

posting

Writing a reply to a message on an electronic bulletin board or discussion.

repurposing

The process of revising training material for use in a different form.

server

A computer processing unit that is shared by a number of users and dedicated to performing specific tasks, such as processing mail and managing print requests.

Subject Matter Expert (SME)

One who is highly skilled and knowledgeable in a given topic.

synchronous

Events that take place together in real time.

Uniform Resource Locator (URL)

A standard way to address any resource on the Internet or on an intranet.

INDEX